THE BOY FROM BIRDUM

THE BILL DEMPSEY STORY

THE BOY FROM BIRDUM

THE BILL DEMPSEY STORY

BILL DEMPSEY

WITH STEVE HAWKE

This is a Magabala Book
LEADING PUBLISHER OF ABORIGINAL AND
TORRES STRAIT ISLANDER STORYTELLERS.
CHANGING THE WORLD, ONE STORY AT A TIME.

First published 2021
Magabala Books Aboriginal Corporation
1 Bagot Street, Broome, Western Australia
Website: www.magabala.com
Email: sales@magabala.com

Magabala Books receives financial assistance from the Commonwealth Government through the Australia Council, its arts advisory body. The State of Western Australia has made an investment in this project through the Department of Local Government, Sport and Cultural Industries. Magabala Books would like to acknowledge the generous support of the Shire of Broome, Western Australia.

Magabala Books is Australia's only independent Aboriginal and Torres Strait Islander publishing house. Magabala Books acknowledges the Traditional Owners of the Country on which we live and work. We recognise the unbroken connection to traditional lands, waters and cultures. Through what we publish, we honour all our Elders, peoples and stories, past, present and future.

Cover Design Jo Hunt
Typeset by Post Pre-press Group
Printed and bound by Griffin Press, South Australia

ISBN (Print) 978-1-925936-04-9
ISBN (ePUB) 978-1-925936-06-3
ISBN (ePDF) 978-1-925936-05-6

A catalogue record for this book is available from the National Library of Australia

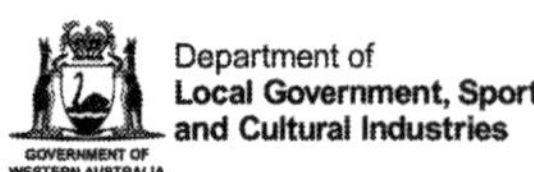

This book is written for my children, Karen, Raelene, Nalita, Marinda and Joshua, and their children.

FOREWORD

I'VE ONLY WRITTEN one book and that was before the turn of the century, 1996 to be exact. There was nothing to it! That's not to say writing a book is easy; it's just that there wasn't too much substance in mine. In hindsight, the greatest achievement of my writing that book was that it was written by hand in South Africa.

I was there for a Test Cricket series between Australia and South Africa. Channel 7 had bought the rights to the series and the late Drew Morphett and I were sent to do the commentary. The cricket was memorable but it was a three Test series that stretched over eight weeks. There was plenty of time to write a book. So that's what I did.

I soon found out that my recollection of events was hardly a mirror image of history. Given I was only forty-seven, and the topic was my own past, things were rarely placed in wrong decades but, then again, only a few memories were spot on.

By contrast, some books demand to be written and read. Unlike mine, they're not written to while away the time. This book is one of those books . . . one that demands to be read. Bill Dempsey writes about matters of consequence. His memory is vivid because he gives matters of importance a face. As you read this book you will come to understand how Bill, throughout a wonderful career, played for three teams, the red and blue of West Perth, the two blues of the Darwin Buffaloes, and the red, yellow and black of his Indigenous peoples. Numerous times his good friends Ron and Stan were on the front line of his defence. These days we would probably label the pair Bill's 'posse' but in those days, they were just 'mates', pure and simple. The irony, of course, is they themselves were outsiders in the outer.

My Dad Jim, and my Uncle Arthur both loved their footy. Jim barracked for West Perth and his favourite player was Bill, but only marginally ahead of Joe Fanchi. The name Dempsey doesn't end in a vowel but on first listen, maybe Dad thought it did, otherwise it's hard to understand Joe's demotion. Both Jim and Arthur were born in Australia. My grandfather had come to Western Australia from Italy as a twenty-year-old. My mother was English/French. The Italian in me was very diluted! I never considered myself a 'real' Italian. Still, the surname was enough for me to get more than a few racial barbs as I played my way through junior footy. Which is not to say I can even begin to understand what Bill and his friends went through, it's merely an observation of Australian society at that time.

I first met Bill Dempsey through Arthur. The man Bill describes in this book as 'a mentor to me'. The pair worked together at Humes, a company once located almost in the shadows of Subiaco Oval. I reckon I was in my early teens and meeting Bill was something very special; he was a living, breathing, real-live league football star. In later life, I remember as a commentator often saying how much Paddy Ryder 'reminds me of Bill Dempsey'. To be fair, that comparison is only partly true because in my opinion, as good as Paddy is, Bill was better. Besides I just wanted to give Bill a mention!

Bill was captain of West Perth for four seasons but what a remarkable roller-coaster ride he had. The club had appointed a new coach in 1973, former Melbourne defender Dennis Jones, and Bill became captain. Jones didn't immediately replace Graham Farmer, he replaced dashing defender Peter Steward who, after only one season as captain-coach, came to the conclusion he'd rather just be 'one of the boys'. It's fair to say 1973 showed little sign of what was to come. Under Jones, the Cardinals were unlucky losers of the Grand Final that year. But things quickly soured at Leederville.

In what I've always regarded as one of the most turbulent years at any club in WAFL history, things spiralled out of control at alarming speed. In this book, Bill doesn't dwell too much on his second season in charge other than to make clear it wasn't one he enjoyed. It's something I knew would have to be in this book. I also knew the year was an extremely difficult one. The club's greatest player and Bill's great friend Mel Whinnen was in Jones' crosshairs. Initially I expected even more venom from Bill. But after reading his account, I reckon he's got it just about right. What's the point? That's not to say Bill doesn't express his feelings here, it's just that he was always one to let his actions do the talking, and starting a disobedience campaign at half-time is a hard act to top. Jones had only the two seasons and was replaced by Graham Campbell, who immediately led the club to a premiership in 1975. It's almost certain Bill's intervention in 1974 made that premiership possible. It also cleared the way for Mel Whinnen to win the Simpson Medal for Best on Ground in the 1975 Grand Final . . . just weeks before claiming his ninth club Best and Fairest.

In so many ways, Leederville Oval and the seven other WAFL grounds around Perth were Bill's natural habitat. He had all the pieces a champion footballer needed to have! He was a natural! Having been lucky enough to watch and 'call' a lot of footy champions over the years, I think the trait that is most often overlooked in champions is courage. Graham Farmer and Barry Cable aren't remembered for their courage. They're remembered for their brilliance. Bill Dempsey was the same. His competitiveness and his willingness to pay the price were too often an afterthought lost in his athleticism and skill. Having said all of that, I've never been one to confuse courage on a football field as a guarantee of courage in everyday life.

All of which leads me to the chapter where he talks about the children to whom he has dedicated this book. I'm sure it took courage for Bill to write it. Even the Coen brothers would have been hard-pressed to come up with such an unexpected detour. But it's a detour that is well worth the trip, even if Bill had to throw his life into reverse to get us there! In this one chapter, I found the Bill Dempsey I've always known on and off the field. The same one my Dad pointed to at Leederville Oval so many years ago and said, 'If you want to become a good footballer, just watch that bloke.' Clearly, Joe Fanchi (a short strongly built Italian rover) didn't fit the expectations my father had for me. In Chapter Thirty-three, Bill is forthright, he is warm, he is funny, he is reflective and, most of all, he is courageous! What's new?

Dennis Cometti

THE DREAM

WHEN I WAS about fifteen years old and still in the mission I began to think about my future. I realised that it was for me to try and work out what I had to do, and plan for the future.

I had to finish high school – Year Twelve. Try and get an apprenticeship – carpentry – so that one day I would build my own house.

Along the way try and play football for the Buffaloes.

Hopefully meet a girl – get married – have some kids – watch and guide them as they grew up, and let the future happen.

So much for dreams.

What follows is Reality.

PART ONE

ONE

I CAN REMEMBER my Dad driving trucks. I was only three years old, but he used to grab hold of me and chuck me in the front seat and I'd go riding with him. My old man, Willie Dempsey, was a truck driver from Alice Springs. But when I was born, in Birdum, he was fighting in New Guinea.

Back then, the rail line from Adelaide in the south ended at Alice Springs, and to connect to Darwin, they had semitrailers carting all the goods to Birdum, which was the southern railhead for the Darwin line. Well my father was one of them semitrailer drivers that used to pull up at Birdum, and he took a fancy to my Mum.

Seventeen she was, Dorothy Holtze.

My grandfather, George Holtze – he was a hard man. He had rifles and revolvers. He said to Willie Dempsey, 'Now, you listen, I know you're hanging around my daughter. See this.' *Click-click* went his gun. 'I'll chase you if you don't do the right thing by this girl.'

'Don't worry George,' Willie said. 'I'm going to do the right thing.'

Anyway, she got pregnant and he got called up in the army.

So my grandfather said to him, 'Hey, remember what I told you.' *Click-click*.

'Don't worry. As soon as I come back, we'll get married.'

He was a sergeant and went and fought in New Guinea.

In the meantime, I was born. It was 1942, when the Japanese were bombing Darwin.

BETWEEN WILLIE DEMPSEY and Dorothy Holtze, my bloodlines cover plenty of bases, you might say.

Willie's father, Jack Dempsey, came from Ireland on a boat, with his brother John. They landed in Melbourne sometime in the early 1900s, as far as I know, and headed straight to central Australia. I used to wonder whether they were criminals of some sort, or maybe running away from someone, but I kept those thoughts to myself.

Old Jack Dempsey had a market garden just outside of Alice Springs. He used to supply the town with everything; watermelons and rockmelons and tomatoes and god knows, and he employed all these Aboriginal people.

Anyway, he met this full blood Aboriginal lady from Utopia Station, an Arrente woman. He did the right thing. He went to the authorities and said, 'I've met this woman, and I've fallen in love with her, and I want to marry her.'

They said, 'You can't marry her, she's a full blood. You just cannot do it, you're a white man.'

But they lived as man and wife, and they had three kids, Willie Dempsey, Lilly Dempsey and Ivy Dempsey. That's where I come from, on that side.

~

ON MUM'S SIDE it's even more of a mix. The Holtze story has all been researched and written up by this lady from the Northern Territory. [*Remember Me Kindly: A history of the Holtze family in the Northern Territory,* Deborah Bisa, Historical Society of the Northern Territory, 2016]

Going right back, my great-great-grandfather is Maurice Holtze. He was a botanist, from Germany. He was travelling around Europe, and he met up with a Russian lady called Evlampia, and she became my great-great-grandmother. They were living in Russia, and some sort of trouble blew up and they had to get out. No one seems to really know the how or the why of it, but they finished up on a boat with their three kids, and they landed in Darwin – or Palmerston as it was called back then – in 1873.

It was a tiny place in those days, and I reckon life must have been pretty tough for those two from the cold country in Europe. There was a gold rush on, but Maurice didn't do any good prospecting. For a while there, he was a warder at the jail. And then after five years, he fell on his feet when he got the job as the 'Government Gardener'. He set up the botanic gardens in Darwin.

Their middle son was a boy called Waldemar. While he was still a teenager, Waldemar got a job with the post office, and then got a posting as a linesman on the Overland Telegraph Line, first to a place called Yam Creek, then to Powell Creek, south of Elliott. The overland telegraph was still a newfangled thing back then, and they had relay stations up and down the line that had been built between Adelaide and Darwin. The linesmen had to relay the messages in Morse code, and they had to look after the lines in their section, repairing any damage.

Not long after Waldemar got the posting, his old man got an offer to go south, to be the curator for South Australian government, to do their Botanic Gardens. He took all of his family, but Waldemar stayed behind. He didn't tell them why. He'd started mingling with the Aboriginal people. He found out that they could have at least five partners. So he said to his parents, 'No, I'm staying. I'm going to be a telegraph man.' And that's what he did. He stayed behind, and he had five wives.

That's my great-grandfather. Wallaby Holtze. The mob couldn't say Waldemar, so they called him Wallaby, and that's what he became known as. He worked for the PMG for most of his life, always in that central area from Katherine down to Tennant Creek. [The Postmaster-General's Department: the predecessor of Australia Post and Telstra.] He never left that country until he was on his very last legs.

Now when I say 'wives', he certainly never married any of them. I don't think they were all living with him at once, like a harem; he just took different women at different times. And one of those women was my great-grandmother Litirngali, a Jingili/Warramunga woman. Wallaby and Litirngali had two boys, Ronnie Holtze, and my grandfather George Holtze.

It's a bit hard to know what to say about old Wallaby Holtze. He became a bit of a legend in the Territory. One of the old-timers. He never really tried to hide that he lived with Aboriginal women and had Aboriginal kids. He used to write letters backwards and forwards with one of those old anthropologists about Aboriginal customs. There was an article in the *NT News* when he passed away that reckoned 'he once claimed to be "overlord" of Warramunga Aborigines at Powell Creek near Newcastle Waters'.

But he never really looked after all his Aboriginal family. Let me put it this way. My grandmother was a full blood woman from Ngukurr, Roper River. She could read and write, taught by the missionaries. But her husband George, couldn't read. His father Wallaby never taught him how.

MY GRANDFATHER, GEORGE Holtze – his tribe was the Jingili and Warramunga people, from the central Northern Territory, around Tennant Creek and Newcastle Waters, all that area. That's where he learned his stockwork. And he was really good at it.

My grandmother was called Alice. Her tribal name was Moondoolooloo. She was a Ngalakan woman. They don't have queens in that area, but she was like a queen. She was very respected, and she was a very tall woman, taller than my grandfather. Very statuesque – a beautiful, strong, black woman.

She was living at Ngukurr, on the Roper River. The Anglican nuns from Groote Eylandt came there and they recognised her, how intelligent she was. So they took her to Groote Eylandt and they taught her how to read and write. When they were satisfied with what they'd taught her, she went back to Ngukurr and she taught all her people, the women especially, how to read and write.

This is the story my Granny told me. George wasn't allowed to marry any of the women available in that area around Newcastle, so he had to go and find a bride somewhere else. He was a law man, a very important man. He got one of his mates and they rode their horses to Ngukurr. He saw Granny. He had his revolvers, and he went and saw the head, the chief, and he said, 'I want to marry that woman.'

'You can't marry her, she's promised to someone else.'

'Well, I don't care about her being promised. I want her.' He waved his revolver. 'You see that? I'm going to take her. If anyone follows me, I'll shoot them.'

So he grabbed her. Took her back to his country.

She went willingly. It is a romantic story. They had eight kids, and they stayed together until the day my grandfather passed away.

HISTORICAL RECORDS SHOW that George and Alice were married in 1919. Their first three children were the girls Dorothy (who would become Bill's mother), Theresa and Rita, born between 1924 and 1927. George found work on various stations in the region, and as head stockman at Roper River, and as a drover.

Through the 1930s, life was a constant battle, not just to survive the Depression years, but to keep their family together. It seems that from 1933, the oldest girl, Dorothy, lived at Birdum in an unofficial arrangement with a Mrs Kearnan at the Birdum Hotel. Whilst they were at Roper River, the two younger girls were taken from them and sent to the Groote Eylandt Mission. George and Alice had to fight for their return.

When they left Roper, Constable Johnson at Mataranka was seeking advice about 'whether I shall remove the lubra [Alice] from the Half-caste [George], also whether I shall take possession of the children [Theresa and Rita] and have them sent to Darwin, also the position as regards the girl now with Mrs Kearnan.'

They entered into written agreements with women in Mataranka to care for their girls whilst George was off droving and Alice working at Elsey Station. But there was constant pressure from local authorities and nosey neighbours for the girls to be removed.

'George and Alice were strong-minded and proud,

and they clearly preferred to keep their family as close together as possible . . . even Constable Johnson was compelled to admit that the family was close-knit.'

At some point in the second half of the 1930s, the whole family, which by now included four young boys, settled in Birdum, where George got work as a fettler on the railway.

[The information and quotes are from *Remember Me Kindly*]

TWO

I KNOW THE story of the day I was born from my Granny Alice.

Old George had somehow got himself a grazing licence. It wasn't a full-blown pastoral lease like the big boys. But it gave him rights to a few hundred acres there around Birdum, to register a brand and to run a few cattle.

It was just beyond the railway station, the railhead there, where all the drovers brought the cattle before they were trucked up to Darwin, and all the trucks from Alice Springs pulled in to put their loads on the train to Darwin.

His brand was GTZ. G for George, and TZ for the Holtze side. He had his three sons working with him at different times. He had horses. And he used to sell his cattle to Vestey's. It wasn't much, but it was something. Sometimes he worked on the railways, and so did my Uncle Angus. They had three shacks there. Corrugated iron, dirt floor, no water, no electricity, no nothing.

There was a big army base in Birdum. The Australian army had a big base there and so did the Americans. And they had the air force there. Their idea was the Japanese wouldn't go that far away from Darwin, so that's where they based their aeroplanes. And there was one pub.

In those days, the beer came up by ship from Perth. They were long-neck bottles, and they used wooden crates with straw to stop them breaking. They'd bring it down on the railway. My grandfather wasn't allowed to drink or go in a hotel. But he went to see the publican, and he said, 'Can I have one of those crates the beer comes in with the straw? My daughter's going to give birth soon, and that's going to be the baby's cot, a beer crate and straw.'

My grandmother told me the day I was born – she's delivering me, see – and she called out to my grandfather George, 'Come on, come here and cut his cord.' So he got his butcher knife out. And my grandmother says to her daughter, my mother, 'Now listen, it's a healthy baby.'

'No, I don't want to know, take it away. Take it away.'

She said, 'Take it away.'

My uncle, mum's brother, and his wife were sitting there watching the birth. So my grandmother sang out to Nancy – her name was Nancy – 'Come over here quick, hurry up. Grab this baby, take him over to your camp and settle him down, while I try to get some sense into Dorothy.'

That's the way my Granny told the story.

Mum was a person who wanted to do the right thing. She was embarrassed that she got pregnant when she wasn't married. I think that is why she didn't want to know me.

So Nancy's sitting down there with me. I was just born, had my cord cut and all that. After a couple of hours I started crying, wanting milk. They didn't have a fridge or anything. They couldn't grab some milk out of the fridge. So Nancy says, 'Mum, this boy, he's crying for milk. We've got to give him milk. You better hurry up, get some sense into that Dorothy.'

Granny finally talked Mum into it, and she finally gave me her breast for milk after about three hours.

~

WHEN THE JAPANESE bombed Darwin, they evacuated all the people from the Northern Territory. We got sent to Victor Harbour in South Australia, me and my Mum and two of my aunties.

I can only imagine how hard it must have been for Mum. My Granny's story makes it pretty clear how traumatic my arrival in the world was for her. Then almost straight away, she is uprooted and sent to country she doesn't know, a single unmarried mother in a time when that was not accepted, and a black one at that.

An Irish lady who ran a boarding house took us in, Mrs Maloney. She found out that Mum could cook – she was a great cook, and her sisters were housemaids. She looked after us, and we stayed there until it was safe enough to go back to Birdum.

I found out many years later that that Irish lady offered to adopt me. It was probably out of the goodness of her heart. She must have figured my future was pretty bleak given Mum's situation. But Mum refused point-blank.

Then Willie Dempsey came back from the war. We went to Alice Springs and Mum and Willie Dempsey got married. They had a baby daughter, Patricia. I was three. We lived in a cottage, renting. But he couldn't even take Mum down to the RSL, you know. They were hard times for my Mum. Willie contracted meningitis, and then Patricia. They died within a week or so of one another.

The Dempsey clan there in Alice knew what was likely to happen. One of the ladies offered to take me in, make me a part of her family, and let Mum try to get back on her feet somehow. Her name was Emma Campbell, she was the auntie of Basil Campbell, who finished up playing against me for South Fremantle. Emma had been a bridesmaid at Mum and Dad's wedding. Mum refused again to part with me; she told Emma no.

But just like the family had feared, the authorities came knocking. They came to my mother and said, 'You will have to vacate these premises. You have no means of support. We're going to have to take your son to Darwin and put him in an institution.'

One fell swoop. She lost her husband, lost her daughter, and they're going to take me and put me in an institution.

THREE

I DON'T KNOW how we got to Darwin. I was probably three and a half. All I can remember is getting to this place on Bagot Road. It was called the Retta Dixon Home. I remember walking in the gates and I just had a little suitcase. I don't know what was in that suitcase, I didn't have much. I just had that terrible feeling that my mother had abandoned me.

When she took me there, I walked in that gate, and I never looked back. The superintendent of the mission, Miss Shankelton, grabbed me by the hand and said to my mother, 'We'll look after him.' She took me and showed me where I was going to – a big dormitory where all the other boys were – and showed me where I was going to sleep.

I just sat there, thinking, 'What am I going to do, what's going to happen to me?' I was so down. I thought, 'Why has all this happened? My mother's given me away. My Dad's died. My sister's died. And now I'm here.' So I just went in.

Slowly, slowly, the other boys that were there, they all came in. 'Hullo,' they all said. 'What's your name? What's your name?' They were all in the same boat as me. I felt good in that way, because I wasn't the only one. But I was really, really upset and broken-hearted.

~

IT WAS A long time before I found out the real story of how brave my mother was, of how she defied the authorities, and exercised what control she could for a woman in her situation. The decisions she made in that awful time, in that nightmare of losing her husband and her daughter, set the course for my life, and made sure that I was not entirely lost to her, as could have happened so easily.

She couldn't stop them from separating us, but she wouldn't let them just take me away. My Mum was a very proud, proud woman. She said, '*I'll* take him myself.'

I can't be sure, but I reckon I know why things panned out the way they did. Back in those days there were dozens, hundreds of kids being taken away from their families, from their mothers, like I was. Most of them finished up in Catholic homes. The Catholics had a place in Darwin. But they also had other places like the Garden Point Mission on Melville Island. Kids finished up being sent all over the place, like my Auntie Ivy. She was sent to Garden Point, and they changed her name to Dorothy. I completely lost track of her until years and years later.

Mum had family in Darwin. She knew how things worked. She knew all the stories. I reckon she figured out for herself that if she let the authorities just take me, I'd most probably end up with the Catholics, and I could finish up anywhere, with her having no say, and maybe never even knowing. That Australian Inland Mission mob though, they just had the Retta Dixon Home. The kids who went there stayed there. And it was right in the middle of Darwin.

She was a fierce and clever woman, my mother. They were going to put me in a Catholic mission. But she wanted to make sure that I wouldn't be lost to her altogether. So she said, 'I'll take him.' And she delivered me to Miss Shankelton at the Retta Dixon Mission on Bagot Road in Darwin so that I didn't go to the Catholics.

I MIGHT HAVE been broken-hearted but I was very, very lucky. There were three girls there at Retta Dixon. Ruthy Snape, Lorna Nelson and Anne Lane. Whether the missionaries arranged it or not, I don't know. But they came and got me and they took turns carrying me around and talking to me and looking after me. I cried for a month. Especially at night, when I felt really alone. And these girls, they never left me. The whole three of them just took it on. In turns. They never left me alone, they were always there.

My sister girls, to this day. I'll never, ever forget them. They were and are such a lovely, precious part of my life. They were only about five years older than me, not even ten. Very young. And they just looked after me. They made me feel like I was wanted, like I was a person. There were all the other boys there, and I'd wonder how they were coping. 'Why am I feeling sorry for myself? I've got these three lovely girls looking after me.' I don't know what I would have done if it wasn't for them.

There was a girls' dormitory and a boys' dormitory. The girls had better accommodation than we did. The boys had these old army huts. Sidney Williams huts they were called. Just a big tin shed. A steel frame and corrugated-iron walls and roof, no ceiling. They used to lock the door at night. But that was pretty stupid. If you wanted to go somewhere, you just opened the window and jumped out.

All you had was a bed. You didn't have your own locker or anything like that. There was a big cupboard, and whatever belongings that you had were in that cupboard, and everybody knew what was whose. We didn't have much, didn't have much at all. That's how we lived.

The bathrooms and toilets were a long way from where we used to sleep. You'd have to walk a long way. No hot water in those days. You'd go down there and take your clothes with you, have your shower, and get ready for bed. They gave us pyjamas, and we had just two sets of clothing, and you had to wear them for two days before they washed them, so you couldn't get them dirty.

A lot of the blokes in the dormitory, me included, used to wet the bed. It was a thing that I couldn't control. And I wasn't the only one, not at all. I reckon about half the boys. And it was a shame thing, because when you did that, you had to get your mattress and take it out and hose it down and leave it in the sun. Everyone knew that you wet the bed.

I was one of those who couldn't control myself for a long while. I think I was about ten years old before I got out of the habit. Me and a lot of other blokes. It was a hard thing to grow up with. You'd think, 'I just pissed the bed again, oh god.' You'd have to go and wash your pyjamas and hang them out, because you didn't want a pissy smell and all that sort of business. So that was a little bit of a shame thing. But you put up with it. I mean, what else can you do?

So that was part and parcel of growing up in the mission until you got to a certain age. And as time went by, you learned the rules. They were Methodist missionaries, and they were very strict people.

They used to teach the girls to sew, and we boys, they taught us how to grow vegetables. You always had chores to do. Raking up leaves or picking up rubbish or things like that. And as you got older, you went to the kitchen as assistants and helped the kitchen people. I remember graduating to the kitchen and thinking, 'How good's this!' It was like Christmas. That was the best job of all because you could eat as much as you liked. We were always hungry.

They had chooks and we used to collect the eggs. But only the missionaries got eggs for breakfast, on toast. We never had that, we weren't allowed to have eggs. Our main breakfast was porridge with powdered milk, and bread and jam. We weren't allowed to have toast. I used to wonder what eggs would taste like, and about how come they could have eggs and we couldn't. It wasn't a big deal, but I used to wonder about it. At night time, it was stews. I remember eating a lot of cabbage. I never saw a lettuce. It was mainly cabbage and potatoes and meat. Very, very average-type food.

The missionaries relied on the government to fund them. There was a subsidy for each kid. I reckon there would probably have been over a hundred kids there.

Mission life. In my book they did a pretty good job. As I got older, it was a good life. You got regimented. They made sure you were clean and tidy, and they made sure you did your chores. And they made sure you went to school.

RETTA DIXON DIDN'T have a good reputation. People used to frighten their kids by saying, 'If you don't behave yourself, I'm going to put you in Retta Dixon on the Bagot Reserve.' Little did they know that a lot of those kids had no choice but to be there. At the time, it was deemed that a lot of coloured people could not look after their kids. They didn't have the means, or their husband had run away. The mothers couldn't support them. So they put them in the Home.

Darwin was a very multicultural society. At Darwin Primary School there were other Aboriginal kids there as well as us from the mission. There were Greek kids, and Chinese. Japanese and white. You name it – they were all there. But us mission kids were the bottom of the heap.

Later on, we used to go by bus. But I can remember for a while when I first started, there was this semitrailer with a mesh cage. This cage semitrailer used to pull up, and all us kids used to get on it. I can always remember pulling up at school, and the other kids would say, 'Here come the Bagot maggots, here they come!' You'd get off, and I always remember, especially the girls, they'd get off and their heads were bowed, they felt that ashamed and embarrassed.

The others would say, 'Don't mix with that mob, they're Retta Dixon people.' It was like people gave us a stigma. I used to always resent that, and I said, 'One day I'm going to try to make it right, where people are recognised and we are equal, just as good as anybody else.' That was a thing with me from when I was a young, young boy. I thought, 'That's what I'm going to do.' I made it my aim in life.

FOUR

MUM STAYED ON in Darwin, getting whatever work she could. She was living out at Winnellie. There was a great big community there. It's all knocked down now, but mainly they were all army huts, the Sidney Williams huts like the one I was in at the mission, from when it was a big army camp during the war.

It was where they put all these people – they weren't rich and they weren't poor, but they were working people. It was a mixture of all sorts; all these coloured people, but white people lived there too, and Chinese and Japanese. It was a place they all went to until they could better themselves, find a better job, or better accommodation. I had aunties there too, and cousins, and all sorts.

Mum used to come and visit me early on at the mission. When I knew she was coming, I'd run away into the bush and hide. On my birthday, she'd bring me presents, and I'd just throw them away. That went on until I was about eight years old. I know I was young, but I think it hurt her as much as it hurt me.

If only I'd known then that twice she'd knocked back people who wanted to take me from her. It was only the power of the government, the authorities, that forced her hand. I did the wrong thing, and it took me that long before I started to realise that it wasn't her fault, that she was trying to do the right thing by me.

But by then, emotionally, the relationship between my mother and me was damaged. From then on, all of my life, I tried to make it up. But face to face, I couldn't. She never ever showed any emotion to me. Which hurt. But I said, 'Well, that's my fault, because of what I did to her,' and I had to live with it.

I'D THROW HER presents away. I'd go in the bush and hide. But she kept coming. She kept coming.

Later on she and her sister even came and got a job at the mission. She was a cook there for a while. By this time I'd got a bit older, and she was in constant contact with me. But the relationship was damaged. And as far as I was concerned, it was my fault.

She was allowed to come and get me out of the mission for the weekends. I'd catch up with my aunties and all my cousins. One of my cousins, David Ross, was in Retta Dixon too by that time. We'd stay with Mum, or with David's Mum, my Auntie Theresa. I was a bit of a cheeky bastard. Mum used to belt me, but she'd only do it to pull me into line.

I was Auntie Theresa's favourite. I can remember her and Mum had a blue one time after Mum had given me a belting. Auntie said to Mum, 'You have David, and I'll take Billy.'

But Mum couldn't keep me there with her because she wasn't married. The mission said you can only have him if you get married. So I always had to go back to Retta Dixon on Sunday afternoon.

FIVE

MUM COULDN'T GET me out of the mission, but I was allowed to go and stay with my grandparents. They were the only ones who could get me out. They didn't have a motor car, but every holiday, twice a year, from when I was young, they'd come up on the train. They'd come up and get me and my cousin David Ross and take us back to their place at Birdum. Right through from when I was a little tacker, until I finished up going to Perth, I spent a lot of time down there with my grandparents at Birdum, and later on at Larrimah when they moved there.

I've got so many stories from those old days at Birdum with them that I hardly know where to start. They hold a very special place in my heart. And I think I can say that I held a special place in theirs. I was the eldest grandson, see. My mother Dorothy, was their firstborn, and I was Mum's first. I was my grandmother's favourite.

But don't go thinking they spoiled me all the time. I was giving my grandmother cheek one day. I did something she didn't like, so she had a go at me. I thought I could get away with it. So I took off. I said, 'You're not going to belt me. I'm going.' Barefoot, hot sand, I'm running from shade to shade to shade. She's got sandshoes on, and she's just walking along with her stick, following me. In the end I gave up.

She gave me a good old whack. 'Don't you ever be cheeky,' she said.

They were hard, tough people. They had to be, the times they grew up in. They had to fight to keep their family together in a time when all the authorities wanted to do was take their kids away. They had to fight, and work their fingers to the bone, just to keep tucker on the table. They were hard, tough people from the old school, but they were good people too. Especially to me.

Over the years, it was hard sometimes growing up without a father. I always wanted to know where I came from. But my grandfather said to me, 'Don't worry about that. You've got no father now. I'm your father. I'm your grandfather and your father.' His advice to me was, 'Whatever you do in life, you do it to the best of your ability. Make a name for us.'

I was only young then. I said, 'Who's going to help me?'

And he said, 'Look in the mirror. That's who's going to help you.'

I've never forgotten that. He was a wise old man, a hard old man. 'You should look in the mirror.'

THEY'D BOTH GROWN up with the Aboriginal law, my grandparents. I missed out on that. They used to start it when you were about fifteen or sixteen. But I was still in the mission, so they couldn't get me to go and do that. I missed out on it, and in some ways I'm sorry I did, I probably would have learned a lot more.

Granny used to tell me stories, all these things about in ancient times in Arnhem Land; the ceremonies they used to do, why they used to do them. Stuff from a woman's point of view. I wasn't sure if she should be telling me some of it. I asked her, 'Why are you telling me all this stuff Granny?'

'Because you're my first grandson, I'm telling you these things.'

There's a story about the time my youngest auntie, Auntie Beryl was born:

I'd gone out with my grandfather and two of my uncles. We were all on horseback. It was dry-season time. We found these cleanskins, so we rounded them up. He wanted to take them back and brand them, as you could in those days. They hadn't drunk for two days, or something like that, they were tonguing for water. Grandpa knew where this waterhole was, so he made a beeline for it.

As soon as they got close, the cattle and the horses smelt the water, and they just bolted for this waterhole. But when we got there, they wouldn't drink the water. We came up, and I said, 'Grandpa, why aren't they drinking the water?'

It was only a small waterhole, more like a pond. In the middle of it was a dead tree. And around that dead tree was curled a big python. Grandpa said, 'Them cattle and horses won't go and drink that water because they're frightened of that snake.'

'Even though they're tonguing for water?'

'Doesn't matter,' he said. 'They won't do it. I've got to go and kill that python.'

He didn't have his rifle. So he jumped off his horse, and cut a sapling, and made a spear out of it. He jumped in the water, went to the tree. He grabbed the python by the head, and he started stabbing it. I couldn't believe I was seeing it. It was a big snake. I thought, 'If that python grabs him, it'll choke him.' Anyway, he killed the python, and then he had to drag it out and take it away from the water. Then all the horses and the cattle drank.

When we got home the next day, my grandmother said, 'George, what did you do while you were away? Did you do anything unusual?'

'What?' he said, trying to act like nothing had happened.

She'd given birth to my Auntie Beryl while we were on the road.

'Come here and look at your daughter,' she said.

Beryl had scars all over her body. They weren't open wounds. Just dark scars.

Grandma believed in reincarnation. She reckoned that Beryl, my auntie, was that snake. Grandpa killed that snake, and all the scars were on their daughter.

I saw all of this. Things like that used to freak me out.

SIX

BIRDUM WAS A hub for all that cattle country, the top end of the Territory and beyond, because it was the railhead for the line up to Darwin where the Vestey's meatworks were. The cattle came in from the Kimberley, from down Tennant Creek way, and in from all those Barkly Tablelands stations to the east.

Me and my cousin David would go and sit on the fence railings at the Birdum trucking yards and watch all these cattle come in. Those yards could hold up to 2,000 head of cattle in one hit, and then they'd go by rail, straight to Vestey's in Darwin. It was fascinating. All the kids in those days used to watch Western shows about cattle drives in America. I had it on my doorstep.

Grandpa George Holtze had lived all his life in that cattle country. His father Wallaby might have been a telegraph man, but George grew up in the station camps, with horses and cattle in his blood. They used to call the men like him shit ringers. Don't ask me why, because they were anything but shit; they knew what they were doing.

I reckon I was about ten the first time he put me on a horse. Me and David, his first and second grandsons. He got these two horses in, and they were big. They just had bridles on, no saddles.

'Alright you two boys, get on those horses. Put your toe where his knee knuckle is, and then jump up.' The horses were moving this way and that, and me and David were packing ourselves. He says, 'Hurry up and get on the bloody horses.'

So we got on the horses and grabbed the reins. He said, 'All right, hang on. If you fall off, get back on again.' And he got his whip and went *bang*, hit the bloody horse. And they just bolted. Me and David were hanging on for dear life. I looked across at him, and he said, 'Don't look at me. I'm trying to hang onto this horse.' And that's how we learnt to ride. Bareback. No saddle.

He was a hard man, but I don't think he was cruel, he was just hard. That's the way he grew up.

I JUST HAVE so many memories of those Birdum days with my grandparents, and nearly all of them are good. Dates and details and the order of things aren't exactly my strong point. It's stories and events that stay vivid in my mind.

One of my favourites is my first killer. It must've been not long after I learned how to ride, I reckon. I don't know where cousin David was that day – maybe he was back up in Darwin with his mum – but I remember what happened as clear as if it was yesterday.

Now anyone who's ever spent any time out in cattle country knows that one of the golden rules is there's no point in eating your own beef. When you go out for a killer, you're chasing either a cleanskin, or maybe a neighbour's animal that strayed the wrong side of the boundary fence.

Grandpa and my uncles knew the score. They'd done it more times than I'd had hot dinners. He gave his sons their orders and sent them off. They knew the deal. Me, I was just following along after Grandpa.

We came to this clump of trees, with the branches all spread out, about ceiling height. We get off the horses, and he's got a sugarbag. He says, 'Climb up that tree.' He doesn't tell me what's happening or anything. I just had to follow orders. Then up he goes too. I'm sitting up there for about half an hour, wondering, 'What the hell are we doing here?' But I didn't say anything.

Eventually I heard this noise. Horses and cattle coming. It was his three sons. They pulled up right underneath the tree. I could reach down and just about touch them, that's how low the branches were. My uncles were just keeping those cattle milling around under the tree.

Grandpa looks at me and says, 'Which one?'

'What do you mean *which one*?'

'You've got to pick a killer.'

'You pick it,' I said.

'Hurry up and pick one.'

'I don't know which one to pick, Grandpa.'

'Just pick one!' he says.

I felt sorry for them. I didn't want to do anything. But I said, 'That one there.'

He's got his rifle – a .22 – and he can reach the bullock from the branch where he's sitting. Right behind the ear. *Bang*. He knocks him over. He gives me the sugarbag and says, 'There's a knife in there. Cut his throat.'

I hit the ground, and that bullock's only stunned. He's getting up. So I chucked the bloody bag, and ran clean up the tree.

'You weak bastard,' he says. 'Go and cut his throat.' But he had to jump out of the tree and get one of his sons to knock the bullock over and cut his throat.

'You'll know better next time,' he said. 'You do that again, and I'll flog you.'

They were the lessons, you know. He wanted to teach me.

AND THEN THERE was my old dog, Butcher. He came into my life from one of Grandpa's mates. Another old shit ringer like him. Coloured bloke he was too. They were like brothers. This old feller won some money and decided he was going to retire up to Darwin. So he came round to see Grandpa and told him about the move and all that, but he was worrying about his dog. 'He's a good cattle dog,' the old feller said. 'I thought you might be able to use him.'

'I'll take him for my grandson,' George said.

Well, me and Butcher were round about the same age, but I was just a kid, and ten's old for a dog. And he'd only ever had the one owner. And at first, it was all growling and snarling from him.

'Just take him around and talk to him, and make him your friend,' Grandpa said.

One day Grandpa said, 'Come on, we'll go and test him out. See how good he is.' He had all these bullocks in the yard, about ten of them, and amongst them was a big bull. He took the dog and me. Butcher's looking at the animals. Grandpa said, 'We'll test him out . . . Butcher, sic 'em.'

Well, Butcher ran through the yard; he jumped through the rails. He went straight for the bull, jumped, grabbed him by the nose and twisted him. That bull fell arse-over.

'That's a good cattle dog!' said Grandpa.

We finally got to be real good mates, me and that dog.

He became my friend. When people came up close to me, he'd growl, as if to say, keep away. He used to protect me. It made me feel real good. I could go anyplace I liked, and nobody could touch me because I had Butcher there.

There was a lot of dingoes around in those days. They used to put the dingo poison up in the trees, not on the ground where ordinary dogs could get them. But Butcher was such an agile dog, he got up the tree and got one of those baits.

He died in front of my eyes. Grandpa said, 'I'll have to shoot him son. I have to. He's suffering.'

I watched him die in front of me.

I thought after that, I'll never have another dog.

SEVEN

I THINK I mentioned before that Grandpa George never learned how to read or write. His father Wallaby never taught him how to. But you know what he used to do? He'd save up all the newspapers. And when I got down there, twice a year, he'd get me to read them to him.

Cover to cover, I'd read them out loud to him, while he sat there smoking his pipe. And if there was an article that took his fancy for some reason, he'd get me to read it back again. I don't know how many hours we spent like that, sitting around the table in the shack there at Birdum.

Thinking back now, I suppose he could've got Grandma to read them out to him. Maybe he did, for all I know. But he probably figured it was good for my learning. And I think he liked to listen to me reading. It was something we shared between the two of us. That's one of the ways him and I got really close.

I never wanted to go back to Retta Dixon when the holidays were over. And they never wanted to let me go. Especially Grandma. She used to say to me, 'You're supposed to be getting on the train to go back, but you're not going on that train, you're staying here.'

'I've got to go back Granny,' I'd say.

'No you don't. Stay a while longer.'

You could see the highway from where they lived. You could see these white cars coming. Those white cars, you knew they were government cars. Grandma or Grandpa, they'd both do it. They'd see those cars, and they'd say to me and my cousin David, 'Quick, jump on those horses and piss off and hide in the bush.' And off we'd go.

Eventually, the police would come. 'That's very wrong what you're doing, Mr and Mrs Holtze. You can't keep them. They've got to go back to the mission.'

We always had to go back in the end.

AND WHILE MY memories of the Birdum days are some of the best that I have, it wasn't all beer and skittles for my grandparents, or, sometimes, for me.

One of the neighbours there was a bloke who was married to a coloured woman from that country. Grandpa knew that woman, and because of that he tolerated the feller, but the two of them didn't get on. I don't want to name him, but this man tried to stand over Grandpa, and he tried to take his land off him.

One time, me and my three uncles had taken the horses to Number Two bore for water. We had to do it every afternoon. It took nearly an hour to get there from our place and then the same back again. This day, we're there at the bore, the horses are having their drink, when around the corner comes that neighbour bloke and all his sons, guns blazing. I thought, 'No, this is not happening.' You would've sworn it was the Wild West in America.

The horses bolted in all directions! And so did we. My

uncles never had any guns. I was on my horse, and I just took my hands off the reins and let him go. I thought, 'I'm just going to have to trust this horse.'

When we got to the bitumen, I didn't know which way was Birdum or which way was Alice Springs. I was so young. I was looking at the road, this way, that way. I just put the reins down again, gave the horse a nice soft kick in the guts, and told him to go whichever way he reckoned. He turned left, and I just let him go, trotting along.

It was getting dusk. We came over a hill, and I could hear a voice. 'You boys, you go back and find him! You find him. Otherwise, don't you come back here! You mob left him there for dead. They could've shot him!'

When I heard her voice, I was that happy. 'I'm home! I'm home!' I grabbed the reins and I galloped in shouting, 'Granny, I'm here. I'm here!'

'You're lucky you boys,' she said to my uncles.

THERE WERE VERY, very few Aboriginal men like my grandfather George Holtze who held a grazing licence, or any sort of land or rights in the pastoral industry back in those days. And there were plenty of squatters and authorities who didn't like him having it.

One time, that same white bloke came and stole a bunch of Grandpa's cattle. Straight out of his yard! Not a big heap, but it was quite a few cattle. And he couldn't stop them. His sons weren't there, only me and my Granny. I saw it happen. The man slaughtered them and sold all the meat.

Grandpa reported him to the police for stealing his cattle and selling them. But the police were on his side because he was a white man and Grandpa was coloured. They said he was telling the truth – 'Forget about it, George, these sort of things happen.'

Grandpa said, 'No, I'm not forgetting about it. I want to press charges.' He went on and on and on, and in the end they had to relent. A magistrate came down from Darwin.

I was there in Larrimah when this magistrate came down on the train. The publican of the Larrimah Hotel met him, and they went back to the hotel where Grandpa's neighbour was waiting for them. They all had lunch, having a good old time. Meanwhile my grandfather, my grandmother and me, we're sitting outside under a tree opposite the pub eating corned beef and damper.

When they've had their lunch, and a few grogs, eventually the magistrate comes out onto the verandah.

'George, come here!'

Like he's a dog.

'I've had a good talk with your neighbour, and he's willing to shake hands, and let bygones be bygones.'

Grandpa said, 'Well I'm not. I'm not willing to do that. I want him charged.'

So the magistrate said, 'Who are your witnesses?'

'My wife, Alice.'

'For goodness' sake George. She's a bloody full blood. We can't take her word. She's not even a citizen. Who else? Have you got anybody else?'

'Yes. My grandson here. He was there.'

'For God's sake! He's a ward of the state George. We can't listen to him, he's only a minor. Why don't you just run along George, and forget all about it.'

He never forgot about it.

That's the way they treated him: 'Run along George, and forget about it'!

And it wasn't just that incident either. The authorities were always giving him a hard time about lease payments, late payments. This, that and the other. Every little thing. That was the shit he used to have to put up with. And he was just an honest man. That's all he was – an honest man working for his family, working to make a living.

I'd look at him and think, 'When I grow up, I want to be a lawyer or something like that; take on these arseholes and the way they treat him.'

For a long time, my plan for when I finished my schooling was that I'd go back and work for my grandfather George, help him out on his block. If things had turned out differently, I might have become a cattleman, not a footballer.

EIGHT

SOMETIMES IT FELT like I had all these different circles of family. They were connected, they overlapped, but they never really joined up.

There was the Alice Springs mob, from my father's side. I knew they were there, but I wouldn't get to know them much at all until many years later.

There were my grandparents down there on the block at Birdum. Blood family. Unquestioning love. From them to me, and from me to them. But that was only twice a year, with those men in the white government cars always on the lookout to stick their noses in if we tried to stretch the days out beyond the time we were allowed.

There was my Mum, living there in the same town as me, but the missionaries and the authorities decided in their wisdom, that it was not a fit and proper thing for a mother and her son to live under the same roof. I got my hopes up at one stage, when she got married. I thought I'd be able to get out of the mission, because they'd always told her that if she was married she could take me out. But that feller didn't want to know about me, and so I stayed at Retta Dixon. Eventually, he pissed off and left her with three kids.

And then there was my Retta Dixon family, my everyday family for ten months of the year. That's what we were. We grew up as a family, a tribe of kids with no parents on the scene, who looked out for each other. The mateship and the brotherhood that came from that family meant everything to me.

Every year the make-up changed. There would be a new bunch of young ones coming in and the older boys and girls leaving. But we all looked after one another. As you grew up, you had to look after the younger mob coming through, make sure they weren't being bullied, or picked on, or teased.

It was like that when I arrived, and those three girls looked after me and it stayed like that. It wasn't something that came from the missionaries. It came from within us kids. That's what you did, that's what was expected of you.

It was something that we had between us. And like true family bonds, those ties amongst us Retta Dixon kids stayed with us for life, long after we'd left the Home. I remember one day me and two of my brother boys were sitting in the Workers' Club in Darwin. The next minute, around the corner come three of our sister girls from the mission.

'Thank god you boys are here.'

'What's wrong?'

'These bikie blokes round there. We just want to play pool, and they're humbugging us and calling us sluts and all that.'

'Really?'

So we go round the corner.

'Excuse me, these girls are our sisters. You've been calling them names, have you? They're our sisters, you don't abuse them. Come outside and we'll sort it out.'

So they said sorry and pissed off.

That's the sort of thing you did. You stuck up for these

girls and you stuck up for the younger kids. You treated them like family.

All through the years that I have lived in Perth, whenever I've gone back to Darwin, which has been every year more or less, catching up with my Retta Dixon family is just as much a part of the trip as catching up with my blood family. I couldn't live with myself if I ever went back and didn't catch up with my precious sister girls, Ruthie and Lorna and Anne.

As the years pass, the ranks get thinner, but still the ties and the memories are strong. I haven't got onto Jimmy Anderson yet, the King as we called him, who played such a large role in my life. But not that long ago now, when he was on his last legs, I was talking to one of the younger boys who'd come into the Home when we were bigger. He was an old feller by this time, into his seventies, but he said to me, 'I remember when you guys used to look after us, you and Jimmy and all of them. You had to look after all of us little boys. When I saw Jimmy there lying in his bed, that memory came back to me.'

WE USED TO do everything together, us kids. Every Sunday, the missionaries would take us to Mindil Beach for an outing. One time, there'd been a big storm the night before, and as we were walking along the beach, we saw that there was this big barge that had been washed up. We were having a good old look over it. One of the kids said, 'Gee, that barge is nearly as big as David Ross's foot.' That's my cousin David, he has really big feet. Well that barge was called Wewak, after the town in New Guinea. From that day on, David has always been known, by me and his mates, as Wewak!

My nickname at the mission was Gudjerdoo. Don't ask

me why, or where it comes from, or what it means. But to this day, if I was walking down the street, and I heard someone say, 'Hey Gudj,' I'd know it was one of the old Retta Dixon crew singing out to me.

Wewak wasn't the only family – as in blood family – who was in Retta Dixon with me. I was the only one who did the really long stint in there, from three years old through to sixteen. Wewak was there for a good while. At different points two of my younger brothers, Dennis and Norman, and my sister Joanie were in there for periods of time. And there were some of my uncles and aunties, the youngest kids of George and Alice. One of them was Freddie, their youngest son.

Freddie was only two years older than me, born in 1940. The missionaries were always telling us that we had to pray, and that if we prayed hard enough, we would get what we asked for. Well Freddie got it into his head that he wanted to test this idea out.

He got some of us kids in and organised this prayer meeting, and then marched us off to the shop. He was bossing us round, telling us, 'No swearing, no laughing you lot. We've got to do this proper way.' Well, would you believe, there by the side of the road, on the way to the shop, one of the kids spots a note. Ten shillings, I think it was. Our prayers were answered! Ice-creams and soft drinks all round, and thank you, Jesus! Us mission kids didn't see treats like that very often, I can tell you.

So we tried it again the next week, and the week after, and the week after. All of us kids praying away, warning each other off if anyone said a swear word. All of that. And then we'd troop off to the shop. But we never did find another ten shilling note, or anything at all, for that matter. And before long the prayer meetings petered out, and we were back to our normal knockabout selves, swearing and all.

ANOTHER ONE, IN my early years there, was Uncle Claudie. He was about six years older than me. Claude saved my life. Literally. The mission had this sort of bush camp set up, a holiday place, up at the far end of Casuarina Beach, the other side of Rapid Creek. It's all suburbs out there now, but back then, it was bush and the odd plantation.

There was something about me and seawater. I nearly drowned three different times when I was a kid. The one I remember most vividly was there at Casuarina Beach, at the camp. Us kids were swimming and somehow I got caught up in a rip. It was a king tide as I recall. I was gone, I tell you, sucked way out to sea, and getting pulled down beneath the surface. I was struggling away but I couldn't beat it. I can remember thinking, 'This is it. I'm gone.' Then this hand grabbed me by the hair, and pulled like hell, and I came up to the surface, spluttering and crying. It was my Uncle Claude. He'd seen I was in trouble, and he swum out and rescued me.

Next time we were down at Birdum, he told Granny Alice about it. Boy, did she give me a talking to. She was a saltwater woman herself, Granny, from that Roper River country. But she made it clear to me in no uncertain terms that I was a desert man by birth and by blood, and that me and the saltwater weren't meant to mix; I should stay away from it. 'The seawater doesn't like you,' she reckoned.

I've heeded her words ever since. I might have lived my life in Darwin and Perth, and both of them are beach cities, but I've never been a beachgoer after that experience and Granny's advice.

NINE

ONE OF THE best things that happened in those years was when Mum got a job at Government House. There was no Northern Territory parliament back in those days – everything was run by Canberra – and the head guy was called the Administrator. He was like the head of the public service but mixed with a lot of the trimmings and ceremonial stuff that a state governor does. And he lived in the flashest house in Darwin, on the Esplanade.

My Mum landed the job as head cook there! She amazed me. She finished up living there on the premises and cooking for all the dignitaries that came through the Territory. I couldn't believe it.

I was still in primary school when she got that job, not far off going to high school, but still living at the mission. She used to say to me, 'Come down at lunchtime, from school. Bring your brothers with you but come round the back. I'll make you all some sandwiches or get you something to eat.'

One day, there were about fifteen of us boys from the mission, all the Bagot maggots, sitting out the back having this great big feed. The Administrator's wife, Mrs Archer, came out the back, and she said, 'Dorothy, who are all these boys here?'

'Well, that boy's my son,' Mum said, 'and these are all his brothers from the mission. From Retta Dixon home.'

'Really?' says Mrs Archer. 'Okay. Now you make sure you give them a good meal every time they come here.'

Well, that's the worst thing she could've said. We were there every day! It only took us ten minutes, and we'd just run, straight from the school to Government House.

I was so proud of my mother. Having a job there. And the extra tucker was pretty good too!

IT WAS AROUND that time – I was still in primary school – when I saw some government people turn up at Retta Dixon to talk to the missionaries. There used to be this big hall there, and they'd put up all these partitions that were about eight feet high, so that you couldn't see in from the outside. I knew something was going on, so once they'd put all the partitions up I snuck in, because I wanted to hear what they were going to tell the missionaries.

Basically, the message was that the missionaries weren't to encourage any of us kids to go to high school. They reckoned that the girls would only end up as domestics and the boys would probably work on the roads or be stockmen. They said it would be a whole waste of education; don't waste everybody's time. I don't know which department they were from, but there were these government people telling the missionaries, 'Do not encourage them to go beyond year seven.'

I couldn't believe it. I was thinking to myself, 'Stuff you bastards, I'm going to high school.' I wasn't especially good at school, but I was determined to get educated. I knew I couldn't get on in this world if I didn't have education. If the worst came to the worst, I was willing to go and work with my grandfather, but there was no way I was going to be a road worker or a run-of-the-mill shit ringer of a stockman. I was determined to have a better life than that.

When I finished year seven, out of my age group at Retta Dixon, there was only me and two other boys who went on to high school. Some of the girls went, but they all pulled out early. And Wewak, but he didn't last long at all.

When we got there the headmaster lined everybody up and told everybody the rules and regulations of being in high school. And all these rules and regulations included wearing a uniform and wearing shoes and socks.

Well we'd never worn shoes, right through primary school; it was always bare feet. So Wewak says to the headmaster, Mr Kissell, 'Excuse me, sir.'

'Yes?'

'What happens if you don't wear shoes?'

'Well, I'm sorry, but that's part and parcel of the rules. You've got to have a uniform and wear shoes.'

So Wewak shook hands and said, 'See you later. I'm off. I can't get shoes.'

He just went. That was his exit from high school. It meant he had to leave the home. He became a ringer and went out droving.

A lot of the boys I grew up with went out and worked on cattle stations as the government people predicted. So when I thought about it, I thought, 'You bastards. You were right.' But I was determined. I said, 'Bugger them. I'm going on, whether they like it or not.'

~

THERE'S ANOTHER STORY from around that time too. It's hard to put things in a definite order this far down the track, but it was certainly after Mum got the job at Government House. It could've been either side of the time I eavesdropped on those government men who wanted to send me out to join a road gang. And it could've finished up worse than a road gang, maybe even worse than drowning.

I reckon I was about twelve, and it unfolded out at that Casuarina Beach camp the mission had. There was an English feller – I'll call him Mister Walls – who had a little plantation out past the mission's camp. Peanuts I think it was.

I don't know how it started. He saw me on the beach, I'm guessing.

Anyway, he comes down to see the missionaries and says he'd like to invite me out to his plantation for a visit. I don't know what the missionaries made of it, but they passed this on. Thank god, I had some sort of radar or instinct switched on. I told them there was no way I was going to his place on my own. But I agreed to go out there if a bunch of us boys could go together. So we did.

I don't really remember, but I don't think it was a great success – us mob of mission boys at the plantation. I got talking to this old Aboriginal woman who worked for him. 'No, he's got no woman, no kids,' she told me. 'No, he never humbugs me; I just do his cooking and cleaning.'

He came back to see the missionaries again. He told them he'd like me to come and visit him again, but on my own this time, not with all the other boys. My radar was getting real twitchy by this time. I told them no way.

But it didn't end there. He went to see my Mum, at Government House where she was working. He spun this yarn about how he was interested in my welfare, and how he'd like to see me become educated, and get on in life. He offered my Mum a big whack of money if she would agree to let him take me to England with him.

Mum told him where to go.

And she told Mrs Archer about it.

Mrs Archer said to let her know if that man ever came around humbugging her again.

That was the last we heard of Mr Walls.

Every now and then, years down the track, when me or Mum were getting on each other's nerves, she'd say to me, 'I should've sold you to that bloody Englishman, you useless bastard!' Me and my Mum – always fighting!

TEN

ON A SATURDAY we used to be allowed out of the mission to go and watch the footy if a parent or a relation came and got you out. They had to bring you back the same day, but you could spend the day there at the Gardens Oval at Mindil Beach watching the games. Whole families used to go along, from all the sides. They'd take all the kids, and lots of tucker, and sit under the shady trees and barrack for whoever they wanted to barrack for. It was just a wonderful atmosphere.

In Darwin we play footy in the wet season. The games run from November through to the finals in March. Back then, in the '50s, there were five teams. Each team would have a bye every third week. Two of them were full blood sides, to use the language of the day. Saint Mary's were the Catholic team. That's the one the Longs and the Riolis have come through. Even in those days, some of the boys would come down on the weekends from the Tiwi Islands to play for Saint Mary's, usually by boat, or sometimes they'd fly. And the local Catholic boys, if they were any good, they weren't allowed to play for anyone else, or they'd get excommunicated. And there was the Wanderers, made up of all the Darwin locals.

Waratahs were a completely white side. And there was

another team called Works and Housing that was made up mainly of white people; they finished up changing their name to Nightcliff. A lot of the boys, coloured boys, who wanted to play with Works and Housing couldn't get a game. So they formed the Buffaloes; 'Bugger you mob, we'll form our own team.'

The Buffaloes' doors were open to anybody. Chinamen, Greeks, you name it. They were the multicultural side. If you were good enough, you'd get a game, no matter where you came from. Mrs Lumlor's lad, Ronny Chin – he was a real fast guy – the Buffaloes' Flying Chinaman they called him. He played premierships for them. George Liveris, who was a big wheel in the Greek community in Darwin – he captain-coached a Buffaloes premiership.

The star of the Darwin competition in the early '50s, when I started going to games, was a feller called Steve Abala. The Buffaloes won four flags in a row, from 1949 to 1952. He was captain for the last two, and he won the league's Best and Fairest medal in the 1950/51 season.

Steve's mother Bertha was a sister to my grandfather George, from old Wallaby Holtze and one of his other wives. When my grandparents came up to Darwin to collect me for the holidays, they'd always go and visit Bertha at her place in Salonika. That was a little suburb close to the city where a lot of Aboriginal and coloured people lived.

I used to sit around and listen to them on these visits. I always remember my Granny saying, 'Now listen George, when we go to visit, you people talk in English. I don't want you talking in your lingo, because I won't know what you're talking about. You might be talking about me.' She had six languages, Granny, and Grandpa had five, but coming from different parts of the Territory, the only one they had in common was English.

But despite that family connection, Mum didn't barrack for Buffaloes. She was a Wanderers girl. And that was fair enough, since two of her brothers played for them.

Steve Abala wasn't just a footy star and a great Aussie Rules player. He was a great rugby player; back then, they'd play Aussie Rules on the Saturday, and he and a lot of others would back up and play rugby league on the Sunday. And he could play basketball, and fight – professional fighting I mean. He worked on the roads. But he was looked up to. He was a leader of men. And he was a handsome bloke. All the women used to drool over him.

Anyway, one day Mum came and picked me up, and we went along with all her friends and relations to watch the footy. We're all sitting underneath a shady tree on the sidelines when Steve Abala comes over. He was already dressed in his footy gear, ready for the game, but he came over because all his girlfriends and relations, all these women were sitting together, my Mum being one of them.

He and Mum were cousins, but he called her sister girl. I was there with Mum while he was talking to her. I was only eight or nine years old. He looked at Mum, and he said, 'By the way Dorothy, sister girl,' and he put his hand on my head, 'I know you're Wanderers, but bad luck – this boy belongs to the Buffaloes.' He was her elder, and she couldn't talk back to him. She wasn't happy but she never said a word.

I was so proud. It was like he anointed me. I hoped that one day I could grow up and be like him, my uncle.

Later on, when I got a bit older, Mum tried to talk me into playing for Wanderers but I told her, 'No way. I'm going to play for Buffaloes.'

My course was set that day when Steve Abala said, 'He's a Buffalo boy.'

> THE BUFFALO LEGENDS invented a way of life that flowed on to the people of Darwin, the Aboriginal people and the mixed bloods. They really were the pioneers that created this way of life. They stood up to be counted. They should be recognised for the guts and determination they showed, which we followed.
>
> *Bill Dempsey narrating the 1997 documentary, Buffalo Legends.*

Steve Abala, who anointed Bill into the club, is one of the Buffalo Legends. He is remembered in the Territory primarily for his sporting deeds. His standing is indicated by the fact that Abala Road, the ring road at Darwin's principal sports precinct, enclosing the TIO Stadium and the Marrara Sporting Complex, is named for him. He is a member of the AFLNT Hall of Fame. He played in six grand finals for the Buffaloes, winning four premierships and two club Best and Fairests, as well as the league Best and Fairest medal in 1950/51.

But the Buffaloes were always more than just a football club. Originally called Vestey's, from the meatworks where many of its players were employed, they rejected that name after the company refused to back the team in a dispute with the league authorities, when the players believed they were being unfairly umpired on racial grounds. In the 1930s, they became the Buffaloes, and their spiritual home was the notorious Kahlin Compound, where people of mixed race from all over the Territory lived under the thumb of the Chief Protector, and the harsh rules of the Aboriginal Ordinance. Even their wages were garnisheed, with the employed men having to request an allowance doled out each Friday at the whim of the Protector.

Abala's father was Bernie McGuiness. His father and uncles played for the club during the 1930s. They were also unionists and political activists. His paternal grandmother, Lucy McGuiness, is said by some to have been the inspiration for Xavier Herbert's seminal 1938 novel *Capricornia*, set in a fictionalised Northern Territory. Herbert had been a controversial superintendent of Kahlin in the 1930s.

Abala joined the army after the Japanese bombing of Darwin in 1942, serving in New Guinea, and volunteering as a member of the Commonwealth Occupation Force in Japan until he was demobilised in 1947. He might have been a returned soldier but he still had to apply for exemption from the restrictive provisions of the Aboriginals Ordinance. Despite clearly being an exceptional man, he could only find employment as a truck driver with the NT Administration. He became an active member of the North Australian Workers Union and helped to found the Australian Halfcastes Progress Association.

As mentioned by Bill, Abala played rugby league as well as Aussie Rules. In 1956, playing for the Navy club, he was kneed in the head in the course of a game. He never regained consciousness and died two days later, at the age of just thirty-two.

ELEVEN

FOOTY AND BASKETBALL were the two sports we played at the mission, and it was mostly basketball, which I loved. Retta Dixon actually had a team that I played in on Saturday mornings. Through primary school, and the early years at high school, the only time I ever played organised footy was at school, the government school kids against the Catholics, but there was no underage competition or anything like that. That was alright by me though, back then I actually loved basketball more than I loved football.

One of the boys at the mission was Jimmy Anderson. He was three years older than me. Jimmy was a natural athlete and a great sportsman. He could turn his hand to anything, but above all, he was a footballer, and a seriously good one. He was a charismatic sort of a feller, even as a boy – a natural leader, and he knew it. I looked up to him like he was a King. All of us boys did. And somewhere along the line, that's the nickname he acquired, 'the King'.

Jimmy had already bailed out of Retta Dixon by the time I reached high school. He'd got himself a job at the Humes factory, where they made cement pipes. And he'd started playing for the Buffaloes. 1954, I think, was his first game. He played on-ball as a rover or ruck-rover. He was small, but nuggety. Fast, skilful, and tough as nails. Tougher than any other player I've come across. 'Hard at the contest,' they'd say today.

He played something like sixteen seasons for the Buffaloes. He was their captain, and at one stage he coached them for a year. He won three Best and Fairests and three flags with them. Like Steve Abala, he finished up being listed in the Territory's football hall of fame, and he was picked in the NT team of the century. But back then in the mid-'50s, when he was starting out, he was just my older brother boy from the mission, and I idolised him.

By this time, I was one of the older boys left at Retta Dixon. I was starting to grow into myself, and I'd become a bit of a leader there, and I suppose I was getting a bit outspoken. The missionaries called me in one day to have a meeting. I asked them what it was about. They said, 'Bill, we want you to make a decision to help your people.'

I said, 'Yes, how am I going to do that?'

'Become a missionary.' They used to do that. They'd pluck the ones they thought had potential and send them away for missionary training. My aunt did it.

I wasn't rude, but I said, 'I think you are asking the wrong person.'

As far as I was concerned, it just showed how little they really knew me, or understood me. They rammed religion down our throats. We had to go, there was no choice. On Sunday we went to morning service, then Sunday school, then evening service. As we got older, us guys used to say that when we left that place, we were never going to go to church again. I was focused on my schooling and my sport. When it came to the weekends, it was the Saturdays I looked forward to, not the Sundays.

And I was really looking forward to starting to play footy with the Buffaloes. I had been since that day that Steve Abala anointed me. But it wasn't that simple. For a start, that year I turned fourteen, even though the league had a colts competition, the Buffaloes didn't have a team in it. That didn't stop us from going down to training with them; they'd pick up me and a few of the other boys twice a week. We loved it.

There was another problem too. There were some boys at the mission who went to play for other teams, and they went straight in and started playing, no dramas. But the missionaries deemed that the Buffaloes were evil. They gambled, they drank, they danced. They fought one another, and everybody else. They would be a bad influence on us. The mission straight-out tried to ban us from joining the Buffs.

At one level, I suppose you could say they were right. The culture of the Buffaloes was about having a good time; work hard, play hard, and when you had to, fight hard. There was plenty of drinking. There was lots of music and dancing that came out of the Sunshine Club days at Kahlin and the Parap Camp after the war, when people had to make their own entertainment because they weren't allowed into the flash dance halls. Most of the fellers could play a guitar or a ukulele.

And yes, they gambled. Pi Cue was the big game. It was a card game adapted from some Chinese game. They played for big money. But it was also how the community raised money when it needed to. The house always took a cut. That was how the Buffaloes raised funds. And that was how we looked after Steve Abala's family when he died. A few big Pi Cue games was how everybody made sure that his wife and kids had a place to live and money to get by on.

There was probably a bit of politics mixed up in it too. Buffaloes were seen as the Labor Party and unions club. And there was a lot of overlap. Steve Abala and the McGuinesses were union men, and the footy club used to always hold its meetings at the Workers' Club in town. I remember the Labor Party always used to take us kids out for picnics twice a year, at Christmas and Easter, and give us little presents at Christmas. There weren't many people in Darwin town showed an interest in us like that.

I reckon if there was two things that defined the Buffaloes culture it was that you look after your own, and you stand up for your rights without taking a backward step. If that's a bad influence, I'll take it any day. And that meant that when us kids told Jimmy Anderson that the missionaries weren't going to let us play for the Buffaloes, there was no way they were going to take it lying down.

They got a delegation together and came to front the mission. Us kids weren't a party to it all, and I'm not even sure who was on that delegation. But I know Jimmy was a part of it. He was only eighteen, but he was already a star. He'd kicked six goals in his first game! And he wasn't going to leave me and the others behind.

I think it went on for a while, there was more than one meeting. When the Buffaloes delegation asked for a reason, the missionaries told them to their face, 'You people gamble and fight and drink alcohol. You'll be a bad influence on these boys.' But the Buffs wouldn't let up. One of them had access to people in the government, and they threatened to take it further. In the end, Miss Shankelton reneged and agreed to let us play. The only condition they put on it was no games or training on a Sunday. 'They're not allowed to come. Sunday is the Sabbath.' But that was okay, the games were on a Saturday. Sundays were for rugby.

~

SO I DID become a Buffalo boy. And the way it all came about meant that I knew I was valued by the club, and my loyalty to them was absolute and beyond any question. The way things panned out, I became known to the world as a West Perth man, a Cardinal. And I am. But before that, I'm a Buffalo. They are my family, just as much as the Retta Dixon tribe are my family, and my mother and my brothers and sisters are family.

I started playing for the colts the year that I turned fifteen, the 1957/58 season. They got their colts team together just in time from my point of view. And in that colts squad of twenty-five youngsters, eight of us were Retta Dixon boys. Jimmy Anderson was our mentor at the club, and our hero.

But I had other mentors too. One old feller in particular taught me many lessons about football and about life. Phillip Snape his name was, but me and everyone else never called him anything but Froggie. He had three brothers and a sister in Retta Dixon and he became like a father figure to me.

He was a working man, like all of the Buffaloes, a garbo in Froggie's case. I'm pretty sure that he was one of that delegation that went and argued the case for us boys at the mission. He was a very intelligent man. Froggie's message was to be proud of who you are. 'If you're going to be a garbage man, be the best garbage man there is,' he'd say.

Give it your best shot – that was his message to me. When you pull the guernsey on, you bust your arse for that guernsey, and the team, and the supporters. You represent all these people, your family, your supporters, the whole lot. So you do your best. That's what I was taught as a kid playing for Buffaloes.

TWELVE

CENTRE HALF-FORWARD was my position when I started out. I was tall for my age and I was a high jumper. I had a good spring. I must have stood out a little bit, because they grabbed me and blooded me early. I got promoted straight into the seniors for a few games that first year, while I was still a fifteen-year-old kid living at the mission, going back and sleeping in the dormitory there after a game. It was tough. But Jimmy Anderson gave us inspiration. 'Have a go,' he said. 'And I'll back you up.' He was our leader, our role model.

If the authorities and the missionaries had had their way, I would've been out bush working as a ringer or a drover's boy, or swinging a pick and shovel on a road gang by this time, but there I was, still at school where I wanted to be, and already playing footy at a level higher than I could've dreamed of at my age.

But I was chafing at the bit at the mission by this stage. And matters weren't helped by the attitude some of them took to the win we had over playing for the Buffaloes. All the boys that were playing footy still had to do their chores on a Saturday morning before they could take off for the day. The guys who played for other teams were told to sweep leaves or rake up, and they'd be laughing at all us Buffalo boys because we were chopping bloody wood.

Miss Shankelton might have reneged and agreed to let us play. Most of the missionaries were fairly decent people, but there were two men there who I would say were not good people, and they were not happy about it. One in particular, who was in charge of us boys. His wife was a lovely woman but he was a really vicious sort of a bloke. Before we went to the footy he made us chop five tons of wood! He hoped it would weaken us but if anything, it made us stronger.

I was more than ready to leave but there was no way it could have lasted anyway. I turned sixteen just after that first season with Buffs, and Retta Dixon didn't let kids stay in the mission beyond the age of sixteen. I actually came and went a bit from the mission that year, staying with Mum's family in Winnellie and what have you, but I couldn't sort out anything permanent. I think Mum was getting a bit worried about me; she reckoned I needed a strong man as a father figure, to sort me out a bit.

And it was her that came up with the solution. She had a connection to this lady Ruby, who she called Auntie. Ruby was married to a whitefeller called Herb Collins. Herb was an old ringer, a tough bastard. He'd come up through the ranks to be a manager of the Works and Housing people who did the roads and all that sort of work. And he was also a good Buffalo man. He was on the committee there, and more or less managed the club. I think he was also, with Froggie and Jimmy, one of the delegation who dealt with the mission for us boys.

Anyway, Mum approached Ruby. She said, 'Auntie, I still can't get him out of the mission myself. It'd be good if you and Uncle Herb could take him in. He's going to get kicked out at some point anyway. They have to leave when they're sixteen.' So Herb and Ruby took me into their family. For the first time since I was three years old, in Alice Springs, I was living in a proper house, as part of a proper family. I was just so happy to get out of the mission.

Their place was in Stuart Park. It was only a few minutes' walk from the Gardens Oval, where we trained and played, so it was real handy. It was a big old-style Darwin upstairs house, but they also had some rooms downstairs and I had one of them. Mum couldn't afford to pay them anything for my board, but Herb said, 'I don't want money, as long as he helps around the place.' And I did, I earned my way, doing all these little things that helped around the house. The thing that Herb insisted on was that I keep going to school. He wanted to be sure I finished my schooling.

THEY WERE LIKE the golden days for me, those times at the Collins'. It felt like freedom. After twelve years of having the door locked on my dormitory of a night in that old Sidney Williams hut, I had my own room. I was a young man about town, free to come and go as I pleased, as long as I pulled my weight around the house and kept up my studies.

Herb used to get on my back a bit – probably on Mum's instructions – he was an old-school ringer by nature. Then Ruby would pipe up, 'Go easy on him, Herb.' He didn't have to put the pressure on me about my schooling, though. I was determined to go as far as I could with my education. So every school day I was there at Darwin High. At lunchtimes, I'd still often head to Government House, where Mum was still the cook, and get a first-class lunch. After school there was footy training and basketball – I hadn't given that up. And I could mix as much as I liked with my family and all my relations, and my mates: all the boys and girls like me who'd come out of Retta Dixon, and the friends I made at the footy club.

One of my best mates from school was Allan Chin. His family was Chinese, Sun Chong Loong, but to make things easier they gave him the name of Allan Chin. He was a good footballer too. They had a restaurant and a clothing shop. Allan used to invite me and a couple of the old mission boys to go to his restaurant of an evening. He said we could eat whatever we want. They'd cook us satays. In those days everyone had their special recipe, and instead of sticks, they used to use fencing wire. They'd put all this meat on fencing wire and cook it all up. You'd kill for it, absolutely kill for it.

When the school holidays came around, somebody lined me up a holiday job at the Darwin hospital in the laundry. I didn't have to work that hard, because I had about five aunties working in that laundry. They were mostly Buffaloes women. They'd feed me up and spoil me rotten, and I was getting good money for a kid from the Retta Dixon Home.

Of a Thursday and Friday night, I'd sell the newspaper too. They were the paydays, when fellers had money in their pockets. I'd head down to the Parap Hotel, and I'd always make sure I didn't have any change on me. A bloke would take a paper and hand me a ten shilling note.

'Oh, sorry, mate. I've got no change.'

'No worries, son, you hang on to it.'

I was shocking, I tell you.

The other way I'd get some money in my pocket sometimes was as a cockatoo. Herb and Ruby would put on Pi Cue nights as fundraisers for the Buffaloes. The games would happen in their house, in the upstairs part. It was all spread by word of mouth, 'There's a big card game at Herb Collins' place tonight.' It was a fundraising thing for the Buffaloes, and also for themselves. Every round, before the winner took his winnings, there was a 10 per cent cut for the house, which would go to the footy club and to them. There was big money changing hands, I tell you.

The games were illegal of course, and they had to pay people to watch out for the cops. The cockatoos. Their job was to give a signal, a knock on the window or whatever, if the cops came anywhere close. I asked if I could do it, and they said yes. Me and my cousin Michael Ah Matt did that cockatoo job, and we got paid five pounds a night for it! Just to give you a comparison, the first job I had when I got to Perth a year or so later, I was getting paid two pound ten for a whole week's work.

MICHAEL AH MATT WAS my basketball buddy. We loved the game, and he was a champion player from a young age. He was the same age as me. He played footy with the Buffaloes, but they didn't have a basketball club, so we signed up to play for St Mary's. That raised a few eyebrows!

The Buffalo mob hauled us up. 'What are you going and playing for them bastards for?'

'Well, where's the Buffaloes basketball team?' we said.

'Never mind that. They're the enemy. You can't play for them, we don't care if it's marbles. You are Buffalo boys.'

But we kept on going. And in 1959, when we were still in school, we both got picked in the Northern Territory side for the Australian championships, playing against all the other states. It was held in Adelaide and we flew down. It was my first time on a plane, my first time outside the Territory.

Michael was just outstanding, so good in fact, that the South Adelaide club down there recruited him. They made him an offer, and he moved down to South Australia and became a basketballer. And he went on from there. He was in the Australian team at the 1964 Olympics. Him and two boxers, Adrian Blair and Frank Roberts, were the first Aboriginal people to make it to the Olympics for Australia. He was in the team again in 1968, but they didn't qualify for the actual Olympic tournament in Mexico.

I was really hoping that I would get picked up along with him from that 1959 championship. At one level I still preferred basketball to footy as a game at that stage. But it wasn't to be; I just wasn't as good as Michael.

So I stuck to my footy. And the footy could hardly have been going better. I was able to cement my place in the senior side from my second season on, playing at centre half-forward. We were a good team, a really good team. We won the flag for two years running, in the 1958/59 and 1959/60 seasons. By the time I was seventeen, I had three seasons of senior footy and two premierships under my belt. I was still underage, but the boys and the Buffalo family celebrated hard, and it was just a fantastic thing to be a part of at such a young age.

THIRTEEN

IN BETWEEN THOSE two flags, in the winter of 1959, Jimmy Anderson had a bit of an adventure. By the end of 58/59, he had five seasons' experience, and he was still only twenty. He was the gun player of the competition as a goal-kicking rover, and a real headache for the opposition coaches. One of those coaches was Jack Larcombe at Wanderers.

Larcombe worked for Native Welfare. They'd posted him up to Darwin from Perth, where he came from. He'd played ten years of senior footy for West Perth. He even won the Simpson Medal in the 1949 grand final. Well he was so impressed with Jimmy that he got in touch with his old club and said, 'There's a guy up here you should bring down to have a look at.'

Now, that was a rare thing in those days; nothing like you see today. Up to that point, the only Territory player who'd made it in Western Australia was Billy Roe from St Mary's, who'd found his way down there and played for East Perth. He was in their 1956 premiership side, alongside Polly Farmer and Square Kilmurray. Pol wasn't one to hand out praise lightly, but one day when we were yarning, he credited Billy with playing a really significant role in that team and that premiership that broke the drought for East Perth. But he busted up his leg real bad a year or two after that. And before Billy, there were two Buffaloes players, Ali Ah Matt and Reuben Cooper, who'd played down in Adelaide.

Anyway, with Jack acting as the intermediary, Jimmy agreed to go down and give it a go. It was a huge deal for us Retta Dixon boys who'd joined him at the Buffaloes. As I've said, we idolised him, and here he was, our hero, off to have a crack in the big smoke.

But being in Perth just didn't agree with Jimmy. He didn't like the weather and he couldn't get used to the lifestyle. He bailed on them, and next thing we knew he turned up back at home. People asked him, 'Why'd you come back?'

He'd just say, 'Why should I stay in Perth? I'm in heaven here at home.' He was just such a happy-go-lucky guy. And he was 'the King' in Darwin.

So he strapped on the boots again for Buffaloes, and we won a repeat flag in that 1959/60 season, with Jimmy at the centre of the action.

BUT THAT WASN'T the end of the story. West Perth were still keen on Jimmy, despite him having walked out on them. He'd made such an impression that they kept talking to Jack Larcombe about how they might get him to come back and have another crack, and how they might work it so that he'd stay the distance second time around. They were saying 'We want this guy, he's got something. We want him back.'

Jack was keen to oblige his old club, and I presume he was also keen on the idea of a Darwin boy making it down in Perth, so he put his thinking cap on, and what he said to West Perth was along the lines of, 'Well look, he grew up on a mission this bloke, and he's a well-known person in Darwin. You can't just take him by himself.' There was two parts to his thinking, I reckon. Firstly, that Jimmy mightn't get so homesick if he had a mate down there. Secondly, he might feel more responsibility if he had a youngster with him.

Now I didn't know Jack Larcombe from a bar of soap, and I don't think he knew anything about me except that I was a young buck who'd played a couple of seasons with Buffaloes and showed a bit of promise. To be honest, I don't even know if it was me in particular that he had in mind, or whether any young feller from the Buffaloes might have fitted the bill. But that thought of his changed my life.

We're at the end of 1959. Cousin Michael is off to Adelaide. I'm still feeling a bit disappointed about not getting any interest from the basketball teams. I'm trying to get through my year ten. Footy season is hotting up, with us the defending premiers, fixed on going back to back. When all of a sudden, there's this talk in the air, that seemed to come out of nowhere, about me going to Perth with Jimmy the King, to try out with West Perth.

Larcombe never talked to me directly. It all came through Jimmy. He started talking to me about the two of us going down to Perth once the Buffs season was finished.

Herb Collins was a bit upset about it. He had some sort of connection with Hec Strempel, who was the secretary of the East Perth club. He'd hooked up with Hec when he came down to Perth on holidays, and there must've been some sort of discussion between them about me. He reckoned that if Perth was on the horizon, I should be thinking about the Royals, East Perth. But he wasn't ever going to stand in my way.

I didn't have a lot of time to think about it all, to tell you the truth. The biggest thing for me was my schooling.

I'd always had it in my mind that I was going to finish high school, go right through to year twelve.

There were so many other things that I had to take into account.

I was happy as a mudlark in the rain, there in Darwin, living the dream life for a young feller, with my mates, my family and relations all around me, and the footy going so well. I wasn't feeling any urge to leave.

There was my grandparents, still down there on the block at Birdum. I sort of knew by that time that I was never going to go down and be a half-arsed cattleman with a grazing licence and a few head of cattle and nasty neighbours. But that didn't stop me feeling guilty and worrying about them. There was that feeling in the back of my mind that I'd be letting Grandpa down.

And I was thinking a lot about my Mum. All the sacrifices she'd made for me. All the difficulties there'd been between us. She had a good job there at Government House. But she had a tribe of kids by then. That feller had walked out on her and left her with the kids. It was always a struggle for her to make ends meet. I felt some sort of responsibility to help her out, and I thought that if I was playing professional footy and had a proper job, I should be able to do that.

Mum wanted me to go. Not for her sake, for mine.

Herb wasn't really pissed off with me. He still reckoned East Perth was a better bet, but in the end, he said, 'Oh, good on you. You go.'

Even my grandparents. I told them I'd got an offer to go to Perth. My grandfather said, 'You go. You go, and you do the right thing by our family. Make us proud.'

I said, 'That's a big ask Grandpa. How am I going to do that?'

And he said to me once again, 'Look in the mirror. That's who's going to help you.'

But I still wasn't sure. I was leaning towards it. I thought I'd missed out on basketball, I might as well have a go at footy. I thought I mightn't ever get another chance. But I had so many good things happening there in Darwin. So many ties that I did not want to break.

In the end though, I didn't really have a choice.

Jimmy said to me, 'You're going. I'm the King, and you're coming with me.' There were no arguments in his mind, no doubts. 'At the end of the footy season, we're going. I'll get onto Larcombe and he'll arrange it.'

And so it was.

We won the flag.

All the Buffaloes mob are still celebrating.

And there's Jimmy with the tickets.

I remember there was a last-minute panic about pants. I'd never worn long pants in my life to that point, but all the boys figured I'd need some in Perth. One of the blokes from the mission, William Lane, he said to me, 'Well brother, me and you are the same height. I just bought these trousers, long trousers. I don't really need them here in Darwin. You take them.'

I'm seventeen years old. Still not an adult according to the law, even if the authorities would have had me out working as a wage slave three or four years ago instead of wasting all that money on an education for an ignorant coloured feller, which was the way they saw me.

I still haven't finished my schooling.

But I've got my first pair of long pants, courtesy of brother boy William, and I'm boarding a Fokker Friendship with the King, on my way to Perth.

PART TWO

FOURTEEN

DARWIN TO PERTH was a different trip back in those days to what it is now. The milk run, we called it, stopping all stations. Wyndham, Derby, Broome, Port Hedland, Geraldton. It took eleven hours. I can remember that old Fokker going up and down like a yo-yo, all the way down the west coast, taking me and Jimmy to a place I knew nothing about.

The words of my grandfather George Holtze were ringing in my ears. 'Do the right thing by our family. Make us proud.' I was determined to give it my best shot, but I had no real idea what to expect.

The West Perth officials met us at the airport, and it was clear to me from the get-go that it was Jimmy they were interested in. I was a bit like the spare wheel, there just as a back-up, and from their point of view, hopefully some sort of anchor to weigh him down in Perth.

It was all a bit of a whirlwind. They got Jimmy sorted, boarding at the Leederville Hotel, right near the ground, and that suited him fine. There was another young feller on their list, Joe Fanchi from the Goldfields, who was staying there too. But I think I presented a bit of a problem for them. I was still seventeen when we arrived. Underaged. They couldn't put me into a pub.

I can't remember how it came to pass, and I certainly don't think I had any real say in the matter, but I found myself unpacking my near-empty little suitcase at a place in Alvan Street in Mount Lawley, just near Perth College. It was called Katukutu.

They were experimenting back then, trying to get Aboriginal boys and girls of mixed race to 'integrate', as they called it. They had these hostels, Katukutu for the boys, and down the road, another hostel for the girls.

There were fifteen of us boys in there and we came from all over. There were a couple like me, trying to make it in the footy world. There were young fellers who had apprenticeships, and others in jobs around the town. We came from all over the place. There were boys from the Goldfields, there were Noongar kids from different parts of the southwest. And there was me, from the Northern Territory. Some of the people couldn't believe I spoke English and knew how to use a knife and fork! I said, 'Where do you think we come from? Darwin is in Australia you know. Up north there.'

We were living in big houses, with house parents, and they were good people. There was only one problem. It was a bloody mission! Those house parents, nice as they might have been, when you came down to it, they were missionaries. We had to go to church every Sunday. I'd just got out of a mission, and I ended up in another bloody one! 'Here we go again,' I thought. I couldn't believe it.

WEST PERTH LINED up a job for Jimmy driving a truck, doing deliveries. The one they found for me was carting furniture. I wasn't that impressed, to tell you the truth. It was ordinary money and bloody hard work, lugging furniture up and down to flats and all sorts of places. I'd finished year ten, and I had plans to continue my education. That wasn't what I had in mind.

But the main thing we were down there for was the footy. We'd missed most of the pre-season, but that didn't matter, we'd come straight out of the Darwin season, and we were fit. We were young, ten foot tall and bulletproof. We fitted in okay.

The coach there was a feller called Arthur Oliver. A real big bloke. He'd been a ruckman and a captain-coach with Footscray in the VFL. 1960 was his first year in the west, as coach of the Cardies [Cardinals], as West Perth were known to their fans. I was a nonentity when it came down to it. It was Jimmy they were watching with an eagle eye. We'd hardly been in Perth a month when the season started, and we both got named in the seconds for that first round.

By round two, Jimmy was named in the seniors.

Steve showed me the *Football Budget* report on that game. 'Little Jimmy Anderson, brought from Darwin by West Perth, lasted only four minutes in his opening game last week. Jimmy made his presence felt with a few promising marks playing on the half-forward line. A little light at ten stone seven pounds, he nevertheless is a quick mover who showed natural marking ability. He twisted his ankle and was thus prevented from showing his ability as West Perth's third rover.'

That's Jimmy. First game in the big league. Only on the ground a few minutes, but 'he made his presence felt'.

I kept playing in the seconds, but that ankle put Jimmy out of action on the field. It didn't stop him making his presence felt in other ways though. He was never one to lack self-confidence. One day after work, he was telling me how he'd been making a delivery in town in his little truck, and everyone started waving at him. He was smiling and waving back at them. 'I'm thinking, I didn't know I was this famous already,' he told me.

And then he realised. He'd gone the wrong way up a one-way street, right there in the middle of the city. They were all trying to stop him and make him turn around. God, I laughed when he told me. 'Jesus,' he said. 'I was so embarrassed.' But he was grinning away because he had a good story to tell.

We were probably in a pub when he told me that yarn. Jimmy liked to do his socialising with a beer in hand. He took me to the Beaufort one time. He'd lined up for us to meet a couple of young fellers there. White boys they were, trying out with Swan Districts, but Jimmy knew them from the footy scene in Darwin.

As soon as they turned up Jimmy sent me to the bar and told me to bring back four beers. I head up to the bar, feeling nervous, because I'm still underage and I didn't want to be getting into any trouble. I'm waiting and I'm waiting, and the barmaid seemed to be avoiding my eye. I'm thinking it's because I look too young. She disappeared, and came back with the manager, and he said to me, 'I'm sorry sir, but we have a policy here not to serve your kind.'

It took me a few moments to work out what he was saying. That sort of thing just didn't happen in Darwin. By the time I did work it out, Jimmy had come up behind me, wanting to know what the hold-up was and where the bloody beers were. So I said to that bar manager, 'Would you mind telling my mate here what you just told me?' So he repeated it. To Jimmy.

Jimmy didn't say anything. He just leaned across the bar, grabbed a fistful of his shirt, and clocked him. Right between the eyes! He went sprawling backwards, with glasses and bottles smashing everywhere! And we went on our way.

All his life, Jimmy knew how to make his presence felt.

JIMMY NEVER PLAYED another game in Perth that year, after his four minutes in round two.

One day he came round to see me and he told me to get all of my money out of the bank. He had his own money, but he'd cooked up a plan, and part of that plan was to make out to me that he was broke.

'What do you want money for?'

'Because I'm going home.'

I was a bit shocked, to put it mildly. All I could think of to say was, 'Hang on a minute, you're supposed to be looking after me.'

He said, 'I'm the King. I do what I want to do, and I tell you what to do. Get your money out of the bank and give it to me. And don't you say anything to West Perth. Don't you tell them until I'm gone.'

Fool that I was, only seventeen, maybe just turned eighteen, I got the money out and I gave it to him.

He hitched a ride north and he was gone.

But before he left, he sat me down, and he told me to do the right thing by the football club that had brought me down here. I was saying, 'No, no, it was you they brought.'

'They also brought you. This is your opportunity. Don't you come back until you make it. If you do, I'll be waiting for you at the airport and I'll knock you out.'

Cunning so and so he was. The reason he took my money

was so that there was no way I could follow him back to Darwin.

It wasn't a saying back then, but it was tough love. That's what it was.

As he said to me years later, 'Everything you've got, you owe me. It's mine. If it wasn't for me, you wouldn't have got it. That car you won – you should've given that to me. The MBE you got – that's mine.'

He had his own way of doing things, the King, but I knew what he meant.

Jimmy was never going to stay in Perth for the long haul. He loved Darwin, and the life he had there too much. But while I might've just been the spare wheel in the club's eyes, Jimmy knew me well enough – probably better than I knew myself at that age – and had enough faith in his little brother boy to reckon that I could make it. So he played his hand in such a way that I had no choice but to stay.

I WASN'T QUITE so forgiving at the time. Imagine how I felt, rocking up at the club on Saturday morning for the reserves game, and they ask me, 'Where's Jimmy?'

'He's not here. He's gone.'

They were left with just the spare wheel.

A kid who's just turned eighteen. Doesn't really know a soul in the whole city. Living back in a mission. A job he hates. And he doesn't have two pennies to rub together because his best mate and mentor and hero has cleaned out his bank account and done a runner.

But I played for the ressies that Saturday and I turned up for work on the Monday.

FIFTEEN

TO QUOTE GRANDPA George Holtze, it was time to look in the mirror.

At one level, it would've been a whole lot easier to just stay quiet, put my head down, and wait till I had enough saved up for the bus fare back to Darwin. I can tell you, I thought about doing exactly that. But there were Grandpa's words, telling me to make the family proud. There were Jimmy's words, threatening to knock me out if I turned up back there. There was Mum's voice in my head, encouraging me to give it a go. And there was a face in the mirror. I was homesick and lonely, but deep down, I didn't want to go back. I decided to give it my best shot, and if it didn't work, then I'd go home.

So I knuckled down.

Once Jimmy had left, probably my best mate during those first few months at Katukutu was a feller called Stan Elliott, who came from the Goldfields. Stan was well-spoken, and a champion bloke. He got a job in the Boans department store in the city, on the shop floor. It was kind of surprising for those days, because Stan was as black as the ace of spades. I think the missionaries at Katukuta must've lined it up for him. He used to go to work in a suit and tie, and all that! He'd say to me, 'Brother, I feel embarrassed.'

I said, 'Why? D'you want to swap with me? I'm carting furniture up and down flats and god knows what, and you're walking around like a silvertail in Boans.'

'Yeah, but people look at me.'

I'd stir him. 'Well I know you're black, but you're not a bad-looking black.' But I told him that I was proud of him.

There was a girls' hostel nearby run by the same missionaries. Same story – they came from all over the place, and they were really lovely girls. Through the week, we'd hang out with them and have a bit of fun, go and have coffee and whatever, and talk about where we came from, or what we were doing down in the city. But come Saturday – especially when West Perth played East Perth – they were all barracking for East Perth. We used to have some good, fun arguments about that, them being fair-weather friends.

Most of the Noongars barracked for East Perth, either them, or some went for Swan Districts and South Fremantle. East Perth were a damned good side. Coming into that 1960 season they'd won three of the past four flags. And, of course, the reason most of the Noongars went for the Royals was because two of their star players were Polly Farmer and Square Kilmurray, two Aboriginal boys.

There were eight league teams, and each one of them had 50 players registered, that's 400 all up. Out of those 400, once Jimmy bailed, there were only five Aboriginal players. Polly and Square. Des Davis at Swan Districts, Irwin Lewis at Claremont, and me at West Perth, and I was a reserves player.

Polly was the out-and-out star of the competition. He had Sandover and Simpson medals, and won most of the media prizes most years. But Square was pretty handy too.

He'd won the Sandover in 1958, and he played centre half-forward, which I still fancied as my position. He was my hero in the competition.

Through that year, 1960, whenever I could, I wouldn't hang around to watch the West Perth seniors after my game in the ressies. I'd make my way to wherever East Perth were playing. If we were both at home it was real easy, we'd be at Leederville Oval, and they'd be just down the road at Perth Oval, where the Perth Glory play soccer now. And I'd watch East Perth play, with my eye always on Square. I never met either of them in those days but I loved watching them play.

That first season I couldn't really get used to the conditions in Perth. I had trouble holding my feet, I'd just fall over. I played out the season in the reserves. But we did win the flag, as did the seniors. It's the only time that has happened for West Perth.

And as the season progressed, I was starting to find my feet, at the club, and in the city. I knew I had to get out of the hostel. That just wasn't a long-term option if I was going to make a life for myself.

There was a family I knew in Darwin. The feller was a cook, a Chinese cook by the name of Cheong Wee. His wife was a white woman, and she had a sister living in Perth. They rang her up and asked if it would be okay if I came and stayed with them for a while until I got organised. So I finished up boarding with this family in Joondanna. And then after a while with the Baulers, I boarded with another family just over the road from them, Ross and Pat McMillan and their two girls. Lovely people, all of them, the Baulers and the McMillans.

And I found myself another job. I didn't want a labouring job. I landed a position as a counter clerk at the Berry

Hardware store in Scarborough Beach Road in Mount Hawthorn. Mount Hawthorn was Cardie country, and when I started working there, people started taking an interest. 'You're the young feller playing for West Perth, aren't you? From Darwin?' They welcomed me, and I started getting to know people. I'm not talking about the club hierarchy, I mean the general public, the supporters. They all took me in, inviting me for dinners and all that. West Perth was a multicultural side. I ate with Slavs and Italians and Greeks as well as everyday Aussies.

Life was busy. But I started to get organised. There was training three nights a week: Monday, Tuesday and Thursday. Games on Saturdays, and then Sunday morning training. And I was starting to feel good. I was independent. I had a good job which I liked. I was happy in Joondanna, catching the bus back and forth. Things started to fall into place for me.

BILL REMEMBERS HIS first year of WA football as being pretty ordinary, and spent in the reserves. In fact, he played six games for the seniors as a freshly arrived eighteen-year-old. His debut was in round six against Swan Districts. And as he mentions, he won a premiership with the West Perth reserves, being named amongst their best players in the grand final. It was his third premiership in three seasons, and his second in the 1960 calendar year, after the 1959 and 1960 flags with the Buffaloes.

Even at that early stage, his career was running parallel with another youngster. Mel Whinnen was six months younger than Bill. He also played the majority of the season in the seconds, but played six games with the seniors, including the winning grand final, where he spent most of the game on the bench, but came on for the last few minutes.

Whinnen won the Best and Fairest count for the reserves, on fifteen votes. Bill finished second, two behind him on thirteen. It would not be the only time this pair, who would become known as 'the Cardie Twins', headed an end of season count over their long careers as teammates.

SIXTEEN

I'D GOT THROUGH my first season in Perth. There were times I didn't think that I would, but I made it. I was very homesick. Very homesick. I'd be on the phone to Mum once a week, and to other friends and family up there in Darwin, so I was always across the news from home and I never lost touch at all but it wasn't the same as being there.

I wanted to have contact with Darwin people. Just about the only one I knew of living in Perth was Billy Roe. He'd stopped playing, after busting his leg, but he was still down here. I'd catch up with him now and then. A lovely feller, and he really encouraged me. He told me that he reckoned I could make it and I should stay until I did.

I even talked one of my old Darwin buddies, David Butler, who I'd grown up and gone to school with, into coming down for a visit. He finished up liking it so much that he organised a transfer with the PMG and he became a postie down here. He's still in Perth today.

And then another Darwin feller came down, Billy Jauncey. He was a year or two younger than me and David. He had family in Perth, but he'd grown up in Darwin, and he was a mad West Perth supporter even when he lived up there. He got a job with Ansett. He started off in baggage services and finished up as their boss for the whole of Western Australia.

I spent a lot of time with David and Bill in those early years, and they are both still mates of mine to this day.

Quite apart from the fact that I couldn't have afforded it, I didn't seriously think about going back after that first season, even for a visit. It would've been too hard to leave Darwin again when it was time to come back, and I just said to myself, 'I'm not giving in.' I was trying to establish myself, to find out whether I could make it work.

The main thing I did over the summer, with some time on my hands, was play basketball. I played in the Bayswater competition. They were good people there but they loved partying! I played for a couple of seasons until West Perth found out and put a stop to it.

I'd go down the beach a bit, but mainly just to watch the girls. I'd jump in and out of the water, to cool down, but I never became a swimmer, thanks to the warning from my grandmother.

And I was thinking about my future. Right from the start, in my mind, making it in Perth was about more than just the footy. I wanted to set myself up for a better life. I'd done year ten in Darwin. Going back to school full-time wasn't an option, but I realised that I wanted to finish off my education. So I went and applied at Leederville Tech, which was right next door to the footy club, and said that I wanted to do accountancy and English, and a couple of other subjects. The accountancy was my own idea. I'd always been pretty good with figures, and I thought it was something that might stand me in good stead down the track, which turned out to be true.

There was no one tapping me on the shoulder or urging me on to do it. It was a bit unusual in fact. Some of the young fellers playing footy were uni students, but most were working men, happy to have a job and play the game. But from the start of 1961, I had another element added to my routine. It became footy, plus work, plus night school.

In the end, I kept the night school going for five years. I didn't get a degree or anything like that, but I passed all my accountancy subjects, and got a real good, practical working knowledge of it. The subject that I did have trouble with was English, but eventually I got there, and got a pass in that too.

That was pretty much the pattern of my life for the next couple of years. I'm not saying I didn't have a social life; I'd started to make some good friends. But I was a busy young man, living in Joondanna with the Baulers and then the McMillans, a full-time job at Berry's in Mount Hawthorn, and Tech in Leederville a few nights a week. All that and the footy. My life was filled up. I felt like I was making headway on all fronts.

WE'RE GETTING INTO the part of my life where my footy career is front and centre. For you footy nuts out there reading this book, I think I better explain something.

I love the game. I owe an awful amount to the game. It is a very large part of what made me the man that I am.

It is what gave me a public profile. I was never very interested in that side of things, but it is why I am in a position now to be telling my story and hoping that there will be some people out there who are interested. But it was never the only thing in my life and not ever the biggest thing in my life. Making my way in the wider world and looking after those near and dear to me are what counted. My family, my mates, and my Aboriginal people – they are who I remember, who I think about.

Willie Dempsey, c.1941
Retta Dixon Home Association, 2009

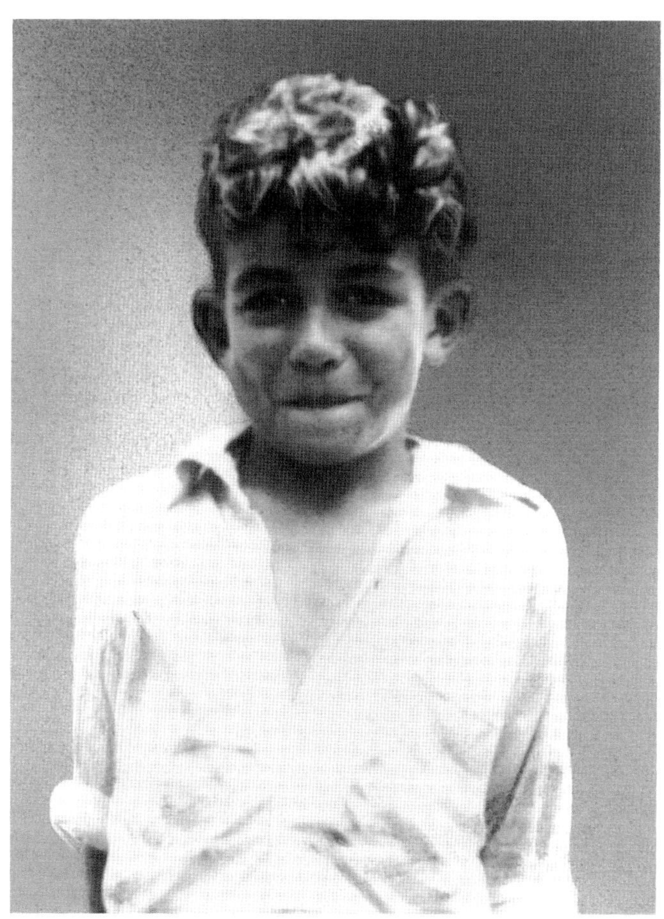

Young Bill *Personal collection*

Retta Dixon children at the beach, c.1952
Retta Dixon Home Association, 2009

Retta Dixon children outside the AIM Church, Winnellie, c.1955. Bill in the back row, far left *Northern Territory Library, PH0221-0278, Retta Dixon Home Association, 2009*

Bill, back right with his mother Dorothy and his siblings Eddie, in Dorothy's arms, Norman, Joanie and Dennis *Northern Territory Library, PH0221-0252*

Retta Dixon Home boy's basketball team, c.1957. Bill, back row left, Wewak back row right *Bill Dempsey per Don Christopherson*

Bill, c.1960 *Bill Dempsey per Don Christopherson*

This family photograph taken by Bill shows his grandparents Alice and George Holtze at the front, and four of their seven children, l to r, George, Theresa, Angus and Dorothy *Personal collection*

Gardens Oval c.1958 Bill in Buffaloes jumper with his brothers Norman, John and Dennis *Personal collection*

Young Bill wearing Grandfather George's hat *Personal collection*

Bill at Leederville Oval, early 1960
Courtesy of Westpix, WAN-0027295

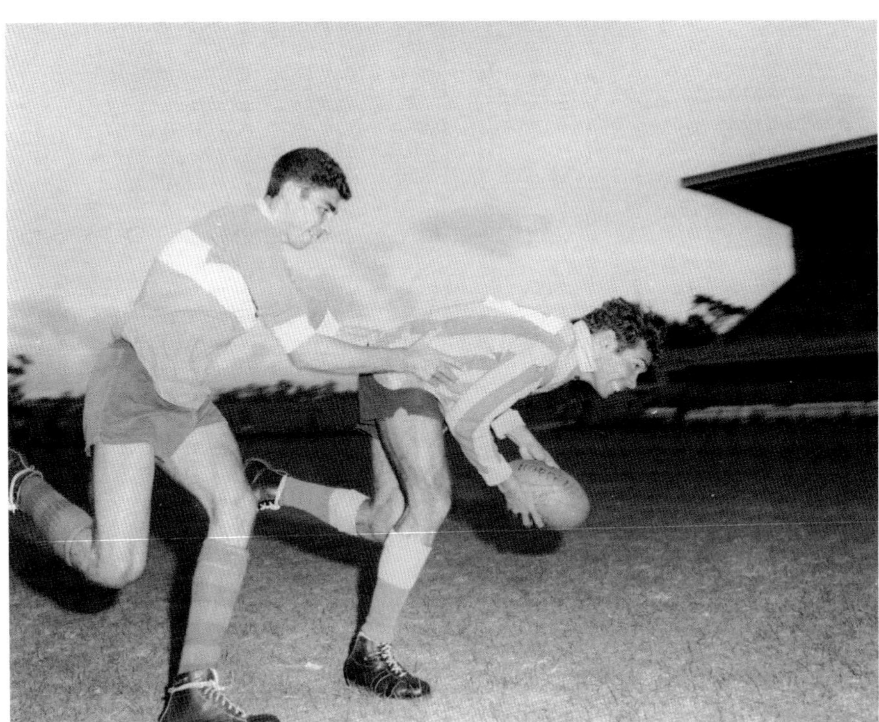

Bill and Jimmy Anderson training, Leederville Oval, early 1960
Courtesy of Westpix, WAN-0027284

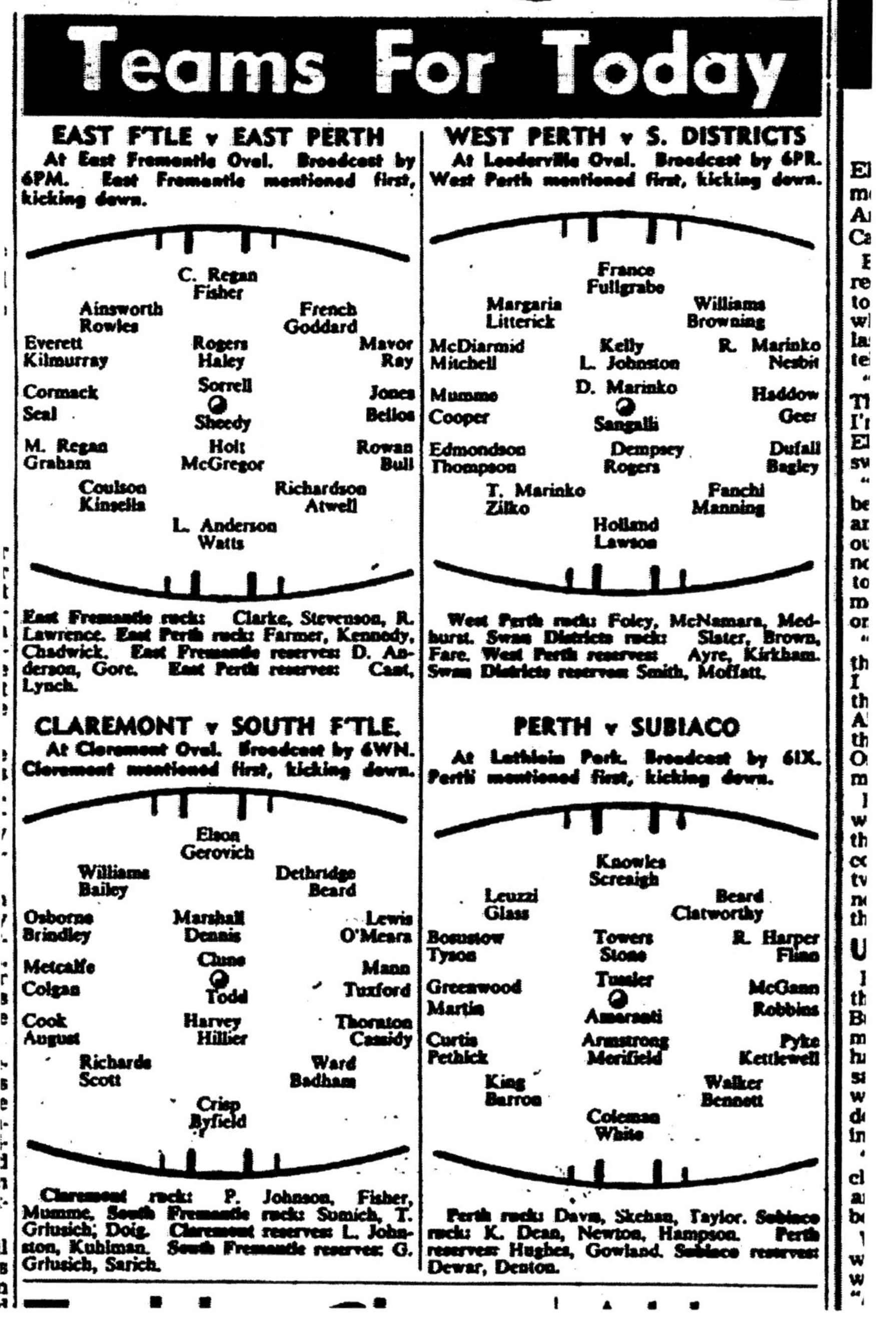

Teams For Today

EAST F'TLE v EAST PERTH

At East Fremantle Oval. Broadcast by 6PM. East Fremantle mentioned first, kicking down.

C. Regan
Fisher

Ainsworth — French
Rowles — Goddard

Everett — Rogers — Mavor
Kilmurray — Haley — Ray

Cormack — Sorrell — Jones
Seal — Sheedy — Bellos

M. Regan — Holt — Rowan
Graham — McGregor — Bull

Coulson — Richardson
Kinsella — Atwell

L. Anderson
Watts

East Fremantle rucks: Clarke, Stevenson, R. Lawrence. East Perth ruck: Farmer, Kennedy, Chadwick. East Fremantle reserves: D. Anderson, Gore. East Perth reserves: Cant, Lynch.

WEST PERTH v S. DISTRICTS

At Leederville Oval. Broadcast by 6PR. West Perth mentioned first, kicking down.

France
Fullgrabe

Margaria — Williams
Litterick — Browning

McDiarmid — Kelly — R. Marinko
Mitchell — L. Johnston — Nesbit

Mumme — D. Marinko — Haddow
Cooper — Sangalli — Geer

Edmondson — Dempsey — Dufall
Thompson — Rogers — Bagley

T. Marinko — Fanchi
Zilko — Manning

Holland
Lawson

West Perth ruck: Foley, McNamara, Medhurst. Swan Districts ruck: Slater, Brown, Fare. West Perth reserves: Ayre, Kirkham. Swan Districts reserves: Smith, Moffatt.

CLAREMONT v SOUTH F'TLE.

At Claremont Oval. Broadcast by 6WN. Claremont mentioned first, kicking down.

Elson
Gerovich

Williams — Dethridge
Bailey — Beard

Osborne — Marshall — Lewis
Brindley — Dennis — O'Meara

Metcalfe — Clune — Mann
Colgan — Todd — Tuxford

Cook — Harvey — Thornton
August — Hillier — Cassidy

Richards — Ward
Scott — Badham

Crisp
Byfield

Claremont ruck: P. Johnson, Fisher, Mumme. South Fremantle ruck: Sumich, T. Grlusich, Doig. Claremont reserves: L. Johnston, Kuhlman. South Fremantle reserves: G. Grlusich, Sarich.

PERTH v SUBIACO

At Lathlain Park. Broadcast by 6IX. Perth mentioned first, kicking down.

Knowles
Screaigh

Leuzzi — Beard
Glass — Clatworthy

Bosustow — Towers — R. Harper
Tyson — Stone — Flinn

Greenwood — Tussler — McGann
Martin — Amaranti — Robbins

Curtis — Armstrong — Pyke
Pethick — Merifield — Kettlewell

King — Walker
Barron — Bennett

Coleman
White

Perth ruck: Dawn, Skehan, Taylor. Subiaco ruck: K. Dean, Newton, Hampson. Perth reserves: Hughes, Gowland. Subiaco reserves: Dewar, Denton.

28th May 1960, Round 6. Bill is named at centre half forward to make his senior debut against Swan Districts *Courtesy, The West Australian*

The earliest pictures of Bill in action, 1961: heading for the goals against Swan Districts *Courtesy of Westpix, WAN-0028819*

Bill taking the mark against East Fremantle *Courtesy of Westpix, WAN-0032331*

There are people who live for the game, live through the game. I know plenty of them. Some of them are my dearest mates. There are fellers who can tell you about the handpass they gave off halfway through the third quarter of a preliminary final forty-five years ago that changed the course of the game. I'm not one of them.

I don't remember my first game for West Perth. This far down the track I get whole seasons mixed up in my memory, let alone the fine details of games. There are a few big ones that are ingrained in the memory but a lot of it is a bit of a blur by now. Some of the details in these pages have only come back to me through the research we have done, with *Footy Budget*s and club reports and press clippings put in front of me. Other stuff I've left to be filled out in the little boxes at the end of some of the chapters.

When the occasion or the need arose, I could talk tactics with my coaches and teammates until the cows came home. But that was to meet the needs of the day, to give my team the best chance to win the game, to win the flag at the end of the year, because that is what we all played for. Once a game was over, I was happy to leave that sort of stuff behind. I played on heart and on spirit, and on loyalty to the club and the supporters who were its lifeblood.

So I'm not the man for an intricate, detailed history of my career, or a tactical analysis of football as it was played in the 1960s and '70s. But I'm guessing you footy fans and Cardie supporters already know this about me.

THROUGH 1961, I reckon I played about half and half reserves and the league side. I was starting to believe in myself. I was a marker, and I had pace. I still thought of myself as a centre half-forward, but West Perth threw me into the ruck.

Froggie Snape, my old mentor, used to say to me, 'Don't you worry about that. Go where they put you. And wherever they play you, bust your arse.' So I gritted my teeth, and knuckled down to become a ruckman.

I was only six foot one and a half, but I was a high jumper, I could spring. I could jump over the top of blokes who were taller than me. These days, Paddy Ryder is one who plays a bit like the way I used to.

I was playing more league games but I'd say I was developing slowly. Every side played four ruckmen back then, two changing out of a forward pocket, and two changing out of a back pocket. There was a pecking order, and at the start, I was number four in that order, starting in a back pocket, and getting called into the ruck when the other feller needed a spell. And when he was ready to get back into the fray, he'd call me out or signal to me, and it was back to the pocket for me.

Brian Foley was the top dog. He was known as Blue. He was the club captain, he'd won the Sandover in 1959, starred in the 1960 grand final, and regularly played in state games. His main back-up was Roy Porter, better known as Lizard. Blue would just come in and tell you to get out of the way. Lizard was a lot better; he'd try to encourage you. You learned as you went, and slowly, slowly you developed.

For some unknown reason, Lizard and his family took me under their wing. He got the nickname because he did actually look a bit like a lizard. He worked in a butcher shop in the Mount Hawthorn shopping centre, near the hardware where I worked. Back in those days you had to work on the Saturday morning before playing the game in the afternoon. Lizard was a character in his own right. He knew everyone around the place, the greengrocers, and the person over the road who had the patisserie. He'd get the best steaks from his shop, and veggies from the greengrocer's, and he'd take them over to the patisserie, and get them to cook it all up. And he'd tell me to walk down to the butcher's after I knocked off. We used to have this big feed and then we'd go to the footy.

One day his boss came in. Lizard and I are sitting out the back, eating T-bone steaks and veggies and potatoes and bread. 'So that's where my profits are going!' says his boss.

Lizard said, 'No, no, we're going to pay for it.'

But the boss told him, 'No, don't worry.' He barracked for West Perth.

MY THIRD SEASON, 1962, was the year that I felt like I really turned the corner. I turned twenty. I was filling out and getting stronger and learning, improving my skills and my ruck craft all the time. I got to a point where I became a regular in the senior side, and had confidence that I could hold my place, and hold my own in the competition.

The team had a better year too. In '61, West Perth slipped back to fifth after the 1960 premiership, but in '62, we made the top four, and got as far as the preliminary final before East Fremantle gave us a hiding. The footy is more fun and the morale is always better when your team is going alright.

That was also the year Jimmy Anderson came back down to Perth, for the third and last time. He had a better crack at it this time. Eight games and seven goals were his stats, and he played some good footy. But it was the same old story, the lure of Darwin was just too strong, and he bailed out well before the end of the season and headed back home. I was sorry to see him go, but this time around was different.

I'd still felt like a kid when I first landed in Perth, and when he left that first time, it felt like I was being abandoned. By '62, I was into my third year of living as an independent young man. I'd found my feet.

By the time that season ended I'd established my spot in the league team, I'd passed the forty game mark, I'd played finals footy. I wasn't a spare wheel anymore and I knew that West Perth wanted me back.

I'd also been away from home and family for three years. It was time to go back and see them all.

THE WAFL HOME and away season consisted of twenty-one rounds, with each team playing the other seven three times. In 1961, Bill played fourteen of the twenty-one games in the senior side. In 1962, he played every game, twenty-three all up, including a first semi and a preliminary final. He finished fifth in the Breckler Medal, the West Perth club's Best and Fairest award, behind Mel Whinnen, who won the first of his nine. He had become a valuable player.

SEVENTEEN

GOING HOME! IT was so good to feel that steamy Darwin air again and to slip back into that easygoing lifestyle. I had the whole summer to reconnect with my old life, and all the people in it. I spent hours yarning about footy with Froggie. I caught up with all the Retta Dixon brother boys and sister girls. My own family of course. I moved around a heap. Some of the time I'd stay with Mum, or I'd just go with the flow of the day, and there was always a bed somewhere at the end of it.

And I started playing with the Buffaloes again. I mean, there was no way I could be in Darwin in their footy season and not pull on the boots for the Buffs.

They said, 'Look, we can't pay you anything.'

I said, 'I don't want money. I'm not here for money. I've come home to play for the Buffaloes. I'm just paying the club back for growing me up and giving me the opportunity when I was a kid.'

It worked out really well for me, being back home, and it made me wonder why I'd ever left.

I was tempted to stay, I can tell you. But it was the same old story. Once the Buffaloes' season was over Jimmy was in my ear telling me to get back down south. Mum was the same. I weighed things up and I knew what I had to do.

So that's how it was. For seven years, 1962 through to 1968. I'd do the season in Perth playing with the Cardies, and then I'd spend as much time as I could back in Darwin with the Buffaloes and with my family and mates. I'd negotiate myself a new contract each year with West Perth and part of the deal was always a return flight to Darwin. The footy season never ended for me and that suited me fine.

The other feller doing a similar thing was David Kantilla. David was a tall, skinny Tiwi Islander who played for St Mary's and then went down to South Adelaide in 1961. He was a ruckman too. When we played against each other in Darwin, the media always used to write it up, 'David Kantilla versus Bill Dempsey this Saturday, come along.' He was a good feller David, and a really good footballer.

THE ONLY REAL interruption in that Perth and Darwin routine came at the end of the 1963 season. West Perth arranged an end-of-season trip to Singapore. That was a big deal back in those days. The planning for it went on for the whole season leading up. I was dead keen. I'd never been out of Australia. But I nearly didn't make it.

On one of my weekly phone calls, I said, 'Mum, while I've got you there, I need to get a passport, so I'll need my birth certificate. Can you send it down to me?'

Silence.

'Hello, are you still there?'

'Yes, I'm still here. Are you stupid or something?'

'No, I just want you to send me down my birth certificate.'

She said, 'Where were you born?'

'Birdum.'

'Who was there?'

So I tell her, 'My grandmother delivered me, and Grandpa cut my cord with his butcher's knife.'

'Was there anybody else there apart from them?'

'Hang on a minute,' I said. 'Don't tell me.'

'The Japanese were bombing Darwin, the army was going backwards and forwards. There was no policeman there, no post office. What were we going to do?' she said. 'Go to Katherine and get you registered? We couldn't do that, because we were all too scared of getting shot by the Japanese.'

'No, don't tell me.'

'Oh, the penny's dropped, has it?'

'I can't believe you never got me registered.'

'I just told you all the reasons why.'

I REALLY WANTED to go on that trip. I told the West Perth officials about my problem, but they didn't come up with anything. And then I had a brainstorm. There was this feller that I knew. He can remain nameless I think, but I knew that he worked in Births and Deaths. So I rang him up. 'Old brother!'

'I haven't heard from you for a long time,' he said. 'Where are you?'

'I'm in Perth playing footy. Listen, I need a favour. I need a birth certificate.'

'You want an extract?'

'No, I want you to create a birth certificate.'

'I can't do that. I'll probably go to jail.'

I kept on at him, promised I wouldn't tell anyone. Gave him all the details: William Brian Dempsey, 17th March 1942, Birdum Northern Territory. Mother: Dorothy. Father: William.

'I can't do it,' he said.

'I thought you were a brother of mine.'

'Jeez, you're asking a big thing.'

Anyway, I talked him round. It was so simple. Hardly even a sentence on the page. He sent it down by mail. I photocopied it about twenty times to make sure I'd always have a copy. And that's how I got my passport.

We did the trip to Singapore. Had a lovely time. Saw all the sights, the Sultan's palace and all that. And we played an exhibition game there. When we got back, I took off up to Darwin. First thing I did was go and see my mate and offer to buy him a drink. 'Buy me a drink!' he said. 'You should take me out and get me smashed, feed me up, the works. I'm still waiting for someone to knock on my door.' But he was good with it in the end.

EIGHTEEN

BACK IN PERTH, I applied for a job at Humes, in the accounts department, and I managed to get it. They threw me straight in as the paymaster in the accounts department. There were somewhere between 700 and 750 blokes on the payroll. It was still pounds, shillings and pence when I started there, and they were all on allowances of different kinds – factory allowances, heat money, enclosure money. I had to calculate all this and have the figures ready every Thursday. There were no computers back then. It was all on one of those adding machines that'd go *ding, ding, ding*.

Humes made pipes. Two different kinds, steel pipes and concrete pipes, so there were two divisions for the company, steel and concrete. I started off doing the concrete division. I got it down to a tee. I knew what I had to do and I had a feel for that stuff. The way it worked, all the workings for the steel division had to be done before the concrete. The other bloke doing the steel used to slow the whole process down and I'd just have to wait. So they finished up swapping us; they reckoned the steel side was harder so they gave it to me. And *bang*, I killed that.

One of the senior fellows there at Humes was Arthur

Cometti. He was the uncle of Dennis Cometti, not that I knew Dennis at that point in time. Arthur took me under his wing and became a mentor to me. He was an East Perth man, but he took a shine to me, and he looked after me at Humes in a big way.

Technically, you were only supposed to get three weeks annual leave, but I'd stay on in Darwin for anything up to three months. I often couldn't get away until mid-November, or something like that, after the footy season had started, but once I was back there, I was there for the season.

West Perth would get onto Arthur and start hassling him about how I had to get back for pre-season training. He'd let me know, and I'd say, 'Just tell them I'm already playing football, I don't need pre-season training.' He'd pass the word on and they backed off. That was another reason I loved playing for the Buffaloes. I used to hate pre-season down here. Hate it. And I was able to tell West Perth, 'I'm training up here, I'm playing. I don't need it.' And if Buffaloes made the finals, I'd tell Arthur, 'I can't come back, we're in the finals.'

Not everyone at Humes was that thrilled with the way I did things. One bloke in particular, who was the head of the accounts department, didn't like it. They used to call him 'Sarge'. He'd get really cranky about it and start kicking up a stink. I was footloose and fancy-free in those days, ten feet tall and bulletproof. I'd say, 'Bugger you, if you want to sack me, sack me.'

More than once Sarge tried to call my bluff. He had the authority to sack me, but he didn't want to do it in his own right, because underneath him was Arthur, and up the line from him was the big boss, Aussie Lovelock. Sarge would go to Aussie and say, 'I'm sick and tired of this Bill Dempsey. I'm going to sack him.'

Aussie would call in Arthur, because he knew Arthur and I were pretty close, and tell him, 'Sarge wants him sacked. I don't want him sacked, I don't care what you do, but you've got to get him back, Arthur.' This must have happened three or four times, but I never did lose my job, and I've got Arthur Cometti to thank for that.

IN 1964, I moved into a boarding house run by an old Irish woman. It was in Loftus Street, just down the road from the West Perth ground and she was a mad West Perth supporter. I'd been with the Baulers, and then the McMillans, but I wanted to be my own man, free to come and go. So, I went to see her, and asked if she might have a place for me, and how much she charged. She knew who I was, and she said, 'No worries Bill, you can move in whenever you like.' And so I did. That Loftus Street boarding house is where I met two fellers who would become mates for life, as close to me as brothers.

Ronny Biok is a Perth boy. His family was Croatian. The name on Ron's birth certificate is Radislav Sardelich, but somewhere along the way, he shortened it. He'd moved over to Sydney and was playing footy over there. West Perth recruited him in 1964 and brought him back home. But he only ever played a couple of games. He was a handsome man, a real good-looking bloke, and he was more interested in the sheilas and in having a good time. He said 'bugger football' and he just chucked it in.

Stan Hart's folks were Irish. They lived in Perth too. Stan was a soldier in the SAS. He was always in Sydney training, or somewhere over there. But he'd jump on a plane and come back home. They'd always come looking for him. We put him on the plane to go back that many times; it's a wonder they never shot him.

Ronny and Stan moved into the boarding house not long after me. It was all pure chance, but the three of us just clicked – the Croatian, the Irishman and the Darwin black-feller – and became the best of mates. We were just three young fellers having a good time, but sometimes we did used to run amok, I must admit. A couple of times, the old lady who ran the place called the cops on us when we were yahooing and playing music and drinking grog. I remember one time, we must've run out of grog, so we all just went to bed. When the police got there, shining their torches and all that, we were all flaked out.

There's no doubt that I was burning the candle at both ends through those years. Looking back now, I don't know how I did it. Ronny and Stan and I were living the good life. And in Darwin it wasn't any quieter. The Buffaloes mob liked to live like there was no tomorrow. The Parap Hotel was the big venue. After a game, most of the team would finish up there and so did a lot of the other teams. They called it the Madison Square Gardens of the north. I was never a fighter but if you wanted to see a fight, that's where you'd go. There was a big open area down either side of the pub and every Saturday night, it'd be on.

I MUST ADMIT to spending a fair bit of time at the Parap, which didn't always please Mum. And that led to one of the stories that has gone down in family folklore. One night I was there with a few mates when the barmaid came over and told me that I was wanted on the phone. I excused myself and went over to the bar to take the call. It was Mum.

'I was wondering what time you were going to be home for dinner.'

'I'm over twenty-one now Mum, you know. I'll come home when I want to.'

I headed back to join my mates, but five minutes later, the barmaid's back. 'That lady's on the phone again for you Bill.'

I excuse myself again, head to the bar again. It's Mum again.

'I just want to know what time you're going to be back.'

'I'll come home when I'm ready Mum.'

This time, I told the barmaid that if that lady calls again, to tell her that I've already left, and I went back to my mates. When I was done, I caught a cab back to Mum's. She was living on a block out at the Sixteen Mile, Howard Springs, with Ike Paterson.

My young brother John saw the cab pulling up, and he came running out, all breathless. 'Bill, Bill, you've got to see this. It's not my fault.'

'What are you talking about, John?' I'm asking, as he drags me round the back. Mum and Ike are sitting on the front verandah, watching, saying nothing. We get round the back and John points at the Hills Hoist, the clothesline. There's a pile of ashes there.

Mum had rung the Parap a third time and got the brush off. She'd sung out to John and told him to get my suitcase that had all my clothes, and every single thing I'd brought up from Perth except the clothes I was wearing. Then she's told him to get some kerosene, and set it alight, right there under the clothesline.

I was speechless.

I went round the front, and Mum and Ike are still sitting there, saying nothing.

'What's the deal?' I asked her.

'All I wanted to know was what time you were coming home, Billy,' she said.

Many, many years later John finished up buying that block where he'd grown up and moving back there. I visited him there one time with Stan, and he hauled Stan round the back, and asked him if he'd ever heard the Hills Hoist story. Stan had, of course, more than once.

'Well, that's the famous Hills Hoist,' John told him. 'The ashes of Bill's clothes are under that grass there.' Stan just cracked up.

I MIGHT HAVE been good at handling other people's money at work, but when it came to my own finances, it was a different story. Up in Darwin, I'd find a few weeks work if I needed to, but mostly I was still getting my holiday pay from Humes. Anything I did have, I gave to Mum, and that was fine by me. In Perth, I'd never have any money by a Monday. Arthur was my banker. I'd go to him, and he'd ask, 'How much do you want, son?' And I'd get enough to tide me over until payday.

He was very good to me, Arthur. And he'd try to get me to see sense. I used to go to his place for dinners, and he'd always be giving me lectures, telling me to stop all my carrying on, and to concentrate on my footy and my work. 'Yes, all right Arthur,' I'd say. And I'd carry on regardless.

The thing was, while I mightn't have been the absolute model employee at Humes, when I was there I did my job and did it well, and through those years of hard living, I never once slacked off on my footy. I kept giving my all, to both West Perth and the Buffaloes.

DEMPSEY'S RECORD AT West Perth in the years 1963–67 is outstanding, in a period where the club itself was middle of the road in the eight-team competition. 1963 was Arthur Oliver's last year as coach and the club just missed the finals with a fifth-place finish. Clive Lewington replaced him in 1964, with the club again finishing fifth, dropping out of the four with a shock loss in the final home and away game. Victorian Bob Spargo then came across for a three-year stint as a playing captain-coach. He took the side to finals each season, losing first semi-finals in 1965 and 1967 and a preliminary final in 1966.

Dempsey played in all but eight games over these five years and some of these were when he was selected for state teams. His first game for Western Australia came in the 1963 season, when he also brought up his fifty games for West Perth. In the four seasons from 1964 to 1967, he finished second in the club Best and Fairest count three times, with Mel Whinnen taking out the medal on two of these occasions. The other year, 1966, when West Perth made it to the preliminary final, he was the runaway winner.

That same year, 1966, he had one of his best results in the Sandover Medal, finishing seventh. And he dominated the media awards, as the West Perth Annual Report notes: 'Winner of Channel 7's Footballer of the Year. 6PR Footballer of the Year and drew in ABW Channel 2's best player of the year.'

By the end of 1967, with the retirement of Brian France, he and Whinnen had become the senior players at the club, with 144 and 148 games respectively. The legend of the Cardie Twins was taking shape.

NINETEEN

AS I SAID earlier, when I started off at West Perth, there was only a handful of Aboriginal players on the league lists. And as was the way in that era, we used to cop it. From the crowd and from the other players. Not all of them, but there were a few in every side that had a mouth on them.

It was bad and it was constant. Every game. At one level, it never used to bother me. Because as my old mentor Froggie used to say, it's the people having a go at you that have got a problem, not you. But you could sense the venom in some of them. 'Dirty black bastard. Don't stand next to me, you stink.' That sort of nonsense. I'd just move in closer to him.

And until I straightened them out, there were some West Perth players just the same. Right from early on, I'd pull them up. If I heard anyone in West Perth doing that sort of stuff, I'd let them know; 'Hey, shut your mouth, otherwise I'll shut it for you.'

Some of them didn't like it. There's a pecking order in a club. But I didn't give a stuff about that. I'd tell them, 'Don't say that in front of me. I'm in your team but that guy is the same as me. If you said that to me, I'd knock you out. So don't call him names.' They knew I wasn't a vicious person but they didn't know whether I would do it or not. If I'd had to, I would've. You can't take that Buffaloes fighting spirit out of a Buffalo boy.

As I got older, people realised that I would always do the best that I can for the club but I didn't tolerate shit. Simple as that. And it started to rub off. As the years went by, I'd hear the West Perth guys telling other people, 'Hey, don't say that.'

There was nothing political about it as far as I was concerned. I wasn't what you'd call a radical, I just wanted to stick up for my Aboriginal people. I was very conscious from early on of the fact that I was the only blackfeller at West Perth. Back then they were rated as a racist club. Noongar people I met would say, 'How come you're playing for them; they're racist bastards.'

'Well, they're the ones that recruited me,' I'd tell them. 'But I'm not taking any rubbish from anyone.'

BY THIS TIME, the latter part of the '60s, as I recall it, there were even fewer Aboriginal players on the lists than when I'd started. Polly was over east. Square had retired in '65. Syd Jackson had done a few years with East Perth and then taken off to play for Carlton. Keith Narkle didn't start with Swans until the '70s. It wasn't because there weren't good players around; there were plenty playing at the lower levels.

I blame the hierarchy of all the football clubs. They were just like all the other institutions and places of employment. Instead of encouraging Aboriginal players, they just saw all the problems and turned away. And if you were lucky enough like me to be a footballer, most of them thought that's all you were good for.

I've got to stress here that I never struck any animosity to me personally at West Perth, and they looked after me very well over the years. I'm talking about the overall attitude of the clubs and the footy world, and the wider community for that matter.

And the flip side of that was the way it made the Noongar people feel. Where I grew up, there was no shame associated with being black. We were taught to be proud of where we came from, whereas here, people were suppressed. I noticed it from when I first came here, there seemed to be a bit of a stigma. People had the shame thing. Some of them didn't like going to training because of that. They just weren't encouraged.

THERE WAS THE everyday racist stuff off the field to deal with too. I'd become well-known so I could walk into a pub and everything would be fine. But then if some Noongar mates came in behind me, you could see the faces change, and the publican would say something like 'I hope you Aboriginal boys will behave yourselves.' That used to get me going, that sort of stuff. I'd tell them where to go and we'd head to a different pub.

And at the games! I'd hear some of it but there was stuff went on that I didn't hear about until years later. Ron and Stan were always staunch sticking up for me, fighting over people calling me coon and boong and all that rubbish.

One day we were playing at Claremont and the two of them were standing in front of a bunch of Claremont members. This bloke in a suit started mouthing off about me. Stan turned round and said, 'Excuse me mate, don't call him those names.' About five minutes later, the bloke is into me again. 'I asked you once mate, in a nice way, don't call him those names.' But he goes again. The third time, Stan just walked up and went smack, knocked him out and broke his nose.

The funny thing about that incident was that a couple of coppers came up to take Stan in, when in stepped this other guy in a suit, and says 'Excuse me,' points at the guy on the ground, 'arrest that bloke for disturbing the peace.' Turns out, he was a detective sergeant who'd witnessed the whole thing. So they carted him away, broken nose and all. I didn't know about this until a long time after; they tried to shield me from all that.

And it even happened in the West Perth clubrooms, if you don't mind. We'd finished a game there at Leederville, I'd got cleaned up and was going to go upstairs to the social hall for a few drinks, but there's my two mates, Stan and Ron, standing at the bottom of the stairs.

'What are you blokes doing down here?'

'Why don't we have a change and go over to the Leederville Hotel?'

'No. This is our club. We go and drink up here.'

'We just thought we might do something different.'

I could tell something wasn't right and I told them to wait there. I went upstairs and saw the head barmaid, Auntie Ethel. 'Auntie, Stan and Ron are downstairs. What happened?'

She started explaining about the rules laid down by the committee that if you throw a punch you immediately get kicked off the premises and wait for the committee to make a decision about whether you'll be let back in. I knew all that; I just asked her who threw the punch.

'It was Stan. I heard everything. This bloke was running you down. Racial stuff. He didn't even barrack for West Perth, and he's up here doing that. Stan was nice about it.

He told him three times. This bloke just wouldn't shut up. He was into you. So Stan shut him up.'

Don't forget, Stan could pack a punch, he was ex-SAS by then, but he was bloody fit and he had the training. After he'd asked him three times and it still didn't stop, Stan just dropped him, right in front of all the committee. None of them had told the feller to shut up. So the president, Len Roper, kicked Stan out.

Once I'd sorted out what had happened, I walked over to the president and I said, 'Listen, two of my mates are downstairs and we're going over to the Leederville Hotel to have a drink.'

'Oh, are you?'

'Yes, because guess what? You kicked them out. And you can shove your club up your you-know-where. I'm off, and you won't see me again.'

Well, they beat me down the stairs to get those two blokes back up again!

I said to the two of them, 'You blokes get me into trouble all the time. I'm becoming the bad boy of this club.'

'It's alright for you,' they reckoned. 'You're just out there playing footy. We've got to put up with all this sort of bulldust.'

TWENTY

AS THE YEARS went by, I became more and more popular with the West Perth fans. Me and Whinney, the Cardie Twins, were their favourites. But it was never like that with the hierarchy, the committee; I was always blueing with them.

The club tried to split me and Ronny up, because they reckoned he was a bad influence. Bob Spargo was the coach by then. I found out years later that he got one of the other players, Gary Ireland, who they'd recruited from Victoria, to spy on us and report back. We caught up not that long ago at the coffee club we have for all the old players. Gary was really embarrassed when he told me about it. But he'd been brought over by Spargo and the club and felt like he didn't have much choice. Not that it made any difference to anything. I was very much my own man when it came to choosing my friends, and most other things.

What used to really get up the committee's nose though, was that I stood up for myself, and I wasn't shy about making sure that I got what I saw as a fair deal. There was no such thing as player agents in those days and a lot of the players just took what they were offered. Not me. Every year at the end of the season, I'd go in and negotiate with them. I'd tell them I wanted a new contract for the next season, and that I wanted X amount of dollars, and of course, my return ticket to Darwin.

I had my ways of putting a bit of pressure on them too. I got to the stage in my career where the Victorian clubs were sniffing around to see if I was interested. I had three different approaches, from South Melbourne and Footscray and Hawthorn. I actually went over once as a guest of Footscray for the finals in Melbourne. They flew me and Ray Boyanich over. But I just had a good time at their expense for a few days. I didn't want to go. I didn't like Victorians, and I didn't like Victoria, and I was happy here. I had a bloody great life.

But that's not what I told West Perth. I let it be known to some friends who knew the committee people that if I got a good offer from Victoria, I'd be going. I said that assuming it would get back to the club, which it did. My mate told them, 'If you don't look after this bloke, he's going to Victoria.' I had no intention of heading east, but you've got to look after yourself in a negotiating situation. One way or another, I did all right out of it each year, partly because I knew how to look after myself, but mainly because I'd become a player that they really valued, even if they would've preferred me to be a bit more subservient.

It wasn't enough to make a living out of in its own right, but by about halfway through my career I was getting good money. But that was only because I persisted. And that is why I wasn't the committee's favourite person.

There's a twist in the tail of that story too. After about five years of this bargaining, one of the committee men let slip to me that everything they gave to me, they automatically gave the same to Mel Whinnen. 'What, doesn't he come and?'

'No, he doesn't have to do anything, because if they are going to give it to you, they are going to give to him.'

He was their golden-haired boy, see.

When I found about this, I said to him, 'Whinney, let's come and sit down, I want to have a yarn with you.'

'What about?'

I said, 'What's your situation as far as payments go, match payments?'

'They just tell me every year how much I'm going to get.'

'All right. Look, I've just come from a meeting with the committee, and I've asked them for X amount of dollars.'

'Oh, right.'

I said, 'Now I want you to go and ask for more than I asked for.'

'Why?'

'I just want you to do it and see what happens.'

'Oh no Bill, I couldn't do that.'

And he never did. He got everything that I ever got, and he had to do nothing. I was the bastard.

Don't get me wrong, that's not a story against Whinney. He's one of my dearest mates; was then, still is now. We are just such different characters. Whinney's an engineer, and a very intelligent man. In all the years we played together, he never ever drank or smoked. He was a clean-cut bloke. Whereas me, I'm a pisspot and a mongrel breed. We're two opposites, completely opposite. They used to call us the Cardinal Twins. We weren't twins at all. One was a golden-haired boy and the other was just a shit-stirrer.

Whinney and I are tied together, there's no getting around it. We started together. We played seventeen seasons together. They even named a stand after us together out at Joondalup where West Perth play now. And the thing is, we clicked on the field together. He knew what I was going to do, and I knew where he was going to be. We didn't talk about it, we just knew. He was one of those once-in-a-blue-moon guys that come along.

But that doesn't mean I don't like giving him a hard time. He was good at pipping me at the post, was Whinney. He got a guernsey in that 1960 flag with a last-minute run on. And I always say he only played that last season in 1977 just to make sure he had the games record ahead of me. And he was always beating me in the Best and Fairest. I managed to win one, but Whinney got nine of them! And I lost count of how many times I came second to him.

I remember one year, a car yard had put up a trip for two to Singapore with $2,000 spending money as the prize for the B&F. That was way bigger than the usual prize. Guess who won it? Whinney. And guess who came runner-up? Me. They presented Mel with his envelope with the tickets and all that, and then they called me up. My runner-up prize was a travelling rug, a red and blue travelling rug. So I made my speech; I'd like to thank you, thank the club, blah, blah, blah. 'And by the way Mel, I'm not travelling. You're going somewhere, so you might as well have the rug too.' The mob just cracked up.

Like I said, mates then, mates still. There was no one prouder or more pleased than me when he got inducted into the AFL Hall of Fame. When I was asked to speak about him when he was inducted, I said, 'How long have you got?' He deserves it.

IT MIGHT HAVE been 1967 that happened. That was one of the years that I finished second to Whinney in the West Perth

B&F. It was Spargo's last year as the captain-coach. We got knocked out in the first semi by South Fremantle. And it was the year young Dennis Cometti, Arthur's nephew, debuted for the Cardies.

As per usual, I made my way up to Darwin at the end of the season and I pulled on the boots for the Buffaloes. That 1967–68 season in Darwin is one of my very favourite football memories. We had a great team, and we had a great year. We went through the season undefeated – the only team ever to do that in Darwin. And we won the flag. And do you know something? Out of the twenty guys in that team that won the '68 premiership, seven of them were Retta Dixon boys. Not bad, hey! It just sticks in my head as more or less the perfect season of footy.

My footy career in Perth is pretty well-documented. There's any number of publications and websites full of records and stats for me and every other player. It was a bit different in Darwin. The Territory has always been a bit more casual when it comes to those sorts of things. That, plus Cyclone Tracy. She blew away a lot of the records, mine and the club's. So I don't actually know how many games I played for the Buffs, but between those early years before I went to Perth, and those seasons in the 60s, it had to have been somewhere over the hundred mark, I reckon – maybe closer to 150.

That flag in '68 was a pretty good note to end on. And as it turned out, although I didn't know it at the time, that 67–68 wet season back home in Darwin was something of a turning point. Those years of burning the candle at both ends were coming to an end.

PART THREE

Bill in a ruck contest against East Fremantle, 1962
Courtesy of Westpix, WAN-0032250

The Buffaloes 1964-65 team, Bill bottom 3rd from right, with mascot T. Nickels
Bill Dempsey per Don Christopherson

c.1964 with David Ross when Wewak came down to try out with West Perth
Courtesy of Westpix, WAN-0027293

Bill and Ron Biok, on their way to the West Perth ball, 1965
Courtesy of Ron Biok

WEST PERTH FOOTBALL CLUB INC.

81st. ANNUAL REPORT

for

Season

1966

Presented to members at the

ANNUAL GENERAL MEETING

Monday, December 12th, 1966.

W. DEMPSEY
Club Fairest & Best
Winner of the BRECKLER MEDAL, 1966.

The cover of the West Perth Football Club's 1966 Annual Report
West Perth Football Club, image supplied by Peter Cutler

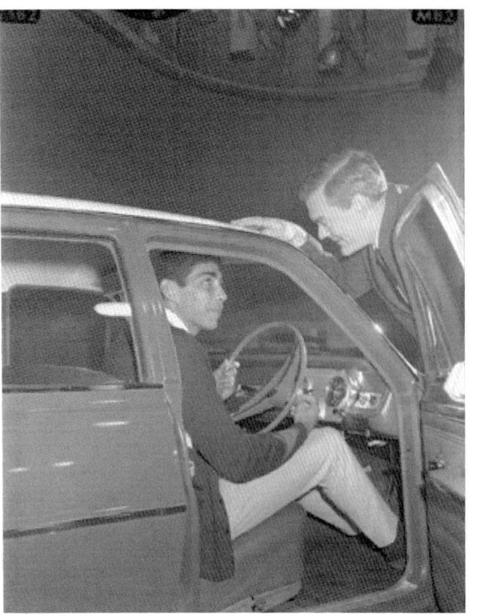

Bill receives the keys to his new car from Channel 7's Frank Sparrow after winning their player of the year award *Source unknown, image supplied by Peter Cutler*

Bill marks against Subiaco, 1967 *Courtesy of Westpix, WAN-0032347*

Bill at the front of a pack crashed by Polly Farmer in the 1968 second semi-final against Perth *Courtesy of Westpix, TWA-0112395*

Bill and Dorothy on the eve of the 1969 Grand Final
Courtesy of Westpix, TWA-0112392

Bill with Stephen Smeath (l) and Bill Valli (r) in the rooms after the 1969 grand final victory *Courtesy of Westpix, WAN-0037099*

Bill at training, 1970s *Courtesy of Westpix, WAN-TWA-0054290*

TWENTY-ONE

I WAS ACTUALLY starting to think about pulling the pin on Perth around that time and moving back home to Darwin permanently. I'd done eight seasons, played just under 150 games, won a Best and Fairest, and played interstate footy. I reckoned I'd done Grandpa proud, I'd done what Jimmy Anderson demanded of me, and I'd been able to help my mother and family out along the way. There was really only one thing missing in footy terms. I hadn't played in a grand final, let alone won a premiership. I did have the Buffaloes flag under my belt after that 1967–68 season, and the two earlier ones with them at the start of my career, but I wanted to play in a grand final in Perth, and I was starting to wonder whether it would ever happen.

Well, everything changed in 1968. While I was in Darwin, the West Perth committee managed to pull off a coup. Bob Spargo had given his notice. They managed to talk Polly Farmer into coming home and taking up the position of captain-coach.

Not everyone at the club was thrilled with the appointment. Every West Perth supporter and player hated East Perth, and vice versa. I hated losing to them. You'd go to

Perth Oval to play them and the hairs on the back of your neck would stand up. You'd grit your teeth and clench your fists and she'd be on. It created good football atmosphere. They were top games to play in. There were people who still thought of Polly Farmer as an East Perth man, but I had an open mind.

As I've said earlier, when I first came down to Perth and was playing in the reserves, I used to go and watch the East Perth seniors play. It was mainly so I could watch Square Kilmurray, but Pol was also a big attraction. He'd taken off to play for Geelong after the 1961 season, when I was still establishing myself, and I don't have any memory of playing against him in those early years.

Of course, I knew all about him. I followed his career. I used to watch him in the replays from the Melbourne comp that were on the telly once a week. In 1968, there was no bigger name in football. But I didn't know the man. I'd never met him.

One of the things West Perth did to try to make the transition as smooth as they could, and to bring the players on board, was to give new positions to me and Whinney, as we were the two senior players by that time. They made Mel the assistant coach. And I was appointed as the vice-captain to Pol.

It is not something that I thought about at the time, and it is not something that anybody commented on back then, but when I was made the vice-captain, it meant that West Perth had two Indigenous men as the captain and vice-captain. This is in 1968, just one year after the referendum that made us citizens, and put us into the census count. As far as I know, in the major leagues – the VFL, the WAFL and SANFL, and more lately, the AFL – that had never happened before, and hasn't happened again since. So you could say we were ahead of our time, and looking back, it is something that makes me proud.

On the other hand, I might have been his vice-captain, but Pol was very much the boss. I've never forgotten our first meeting.

At West Perth, we always had what we used to call a pleasant Sunday morning. It was actually just a piss-up; a short training run and then everyone would have a few drinks. But this one was different. It was Pol's introduction to the players, and our introduction to him. The whole team was there, everybody on the list. All the committee. And a lot of the members.

Pol had done his homework. He had a dossier on each player. He was going through, reading the names, saying what he knew of them and what he expected. My dossier must have had a fair bit in it, all my escapades with Ronny and Stan and what have you. He got to me, and he said, 'Bill Dempsey. Drinks, smokes, and hates training.' Short and sweet, but true I must admit. And then he said, 'And the first bad game he plays, I'm going to drop him.'

So I stood up, and I said, 'Don't hold your breath.' That was my introduction to Pol. We shook hands and we got on with the business.

From the start, I told Pol, 'You can do whatever you like with these blokes, train us however you like. But I come from tradition. I only played for one footy club, Buffaloes. And this is my second club. I was taught in the old way, that you bust your arse for the club, you bust your arse for the team. That's what you do. It doesn't matter who the coach is – that's it – you give it your best shot, and I'm telling you the same.' I told him, 'You don't have to stand over me, I know what to do.' That was our introduction. I was up-front with him and he was up-front with me.

POLLY FARMER WAS not only a gun footballer, he was a gun coach, as far as I was concerned. Bob Spargo deserves a lot of credit for building that team over the three years he was there, with the young players he brought in, and the way he developed them, but Pol took us to another level.

The training days were upped to Monday through to Thursday, plus the Sunday morning sessions. So we used to only have one day off training – that was Friday. A couple of the blokes complained that they had to work, they couldn't make a living just out of footy. But for Pol, footy always came first, and he expected the same of us. 'You've got to show dedication to your club,' he'd say. 'And to yourself as a sportsman.' He reckoned that if we were fair dinkum, we'd call in to the club on the Friday on the way home from work and do ten laps. That's how strict he was. But I wasn't doing that. I wanted one night off.

People say, 'You blokes weren't really fit in those days.' We were fit, I tell you. We were the fittest guys ever, in that era; at West Perth we were, anyway. We'd run through a brick wall. And the training and drills were intense and competitive. At kick-to-kick, if the ball spilled, you were expected to follow-up and compete on the ground, as fiercely as if it was a game. We all became better kicks, and we all had to follow Pol's golden rule. Kick it to the advantage of your teammate.

And above all, he toughened us up, especially us big guys. One day we arrived at training, and there was this big contraption with a metal arm that swung out onto the oval, and there was this big punching bag hanging from it. He got all the ruckmen and the other big blokes, and one by one, we had to grab onto that bag, hang onto it for dear life like it was the ball. And every single bloke on the training list – fifty blokes – had to go back twenty metres, run through, and hit that bag as hard as they could. Pol would tell them, 'See how far back you can put the bloke with the bag.' It was like being hit by a freight train. No rest in between. They'd just keep coming. *Bang. Bang. Bang.* Then the next big bloke would take his turn. Pol included. And everyone on the list would try to run through that feller. Fair dinkum, it felt like being in the ring with Sonny Liston or Joe Louis. That became part of the training routine every night.

I was playing at fourteen and a half to fifteen stone in those days. And it was all muscle. From that punching bag, and playing all the time, you got really tough. I felt like if you hit me with a stick, it was the stick that'd break.

That toughness he put into us wasn't just for its own sake. Polly expected us to use it. For instance, we had a bloke called Stephen Smeath. We used to call him the Road Runner. He was built like a bone-arsed kangaroo dog, there was bugger all of him. And he could run. Other sides used to call him gutless and a front runner. He wasn't a fighter, but he was one of the bravest blokes I ever saw play football. Every time he ran out on the ground, there were eighteen opposition players who wanted to kill him. I'll stand up and sing his praises any day.

Pol said our job – especially him and me, but all the big ruckmen – was to look after Smeath. 'If anyone touches him, you've got to put them down. And when you kick the ball to Smeath, if he has to prop and lean back and wait for the mob to come and smash him, I'll take you off the ground.' Our instructions were that if you couldn't hit him with a pass, you put it on the ground in front of him, and he'd do the rest. No one could catch him.

I could never work out why the opposition hated Smeathy so much, he was a ball player. But they did. There was an East Perth guy who used to work at the same place as me. One day in the lunchroom he said to me, 'I'm glad we're playing you guys this week. The first chance I get, I'm going to kill Stephen Smeath.'

I said, 'Do you know him?'

'No, but he's a wimp and a show-off.'

'You don't even know the guy, but you're going to go out and deliberately maim someone?'

He told me how he was going to do it. He reckoned he knew how he played. 'He just runs on the outside and you blokes feed it out to him. I'm going to catch him when he does that.'

In the game, I could see it developing. Smeathy was on the half-back flank. Me and Polly were in the pack. This bloke took off. I knew exactly what was going to happen. He was going to put Stephen into the grandstand. As Smeathy grabbed the ball and took off, this bloke was lying on the ground with his ribs caved in. He'd just run straight into my elbow. I didn't hit him. I just went out and met him before he met Smeathy. He was lying there calling me all sorts.

'Remember what you said in the lunchroom? I forgot to tell you, Smeathy's my mate.'

I was always a ball player but I played hard. There was no point being soft about it. And like Pol, I reckoned it was my job to protect the little blokes in our team, always.

That was a bit of a sidetrack. But it's an example of what we were about as a team during those years under Polly. He got us fit. He toughened us up. He got us playing smart and playing to a system. He made us better footballers individually, and a better team.

Above all, Pol hated losing. Hated it. Despised it. He said, 'If we can win by one point, I'll be happy. If we can win by a hundred points, I'll be even happier. Give them nothing. When you get them on the run, kill them.'

He wasn't a fire and brimstone sort of guy. He was a psychologist. He could work out people and players, and how to get the best out of them. He wasn't beyond riling me up on purpose if he thought it was needed on the day. He was a phenomenal coach. I can't speak highly enough of him.

That first year under Polly, 1968, we played some great footy. Right through the season, we were up the top in first or second place. We knew we had a good side. We should have made the grand final. We should really have won it I reckon. But we couldn't finish it off. We bombed out; lost both of our finals, to Perth and then East Perth. Close, but not close enough.

That was a big let-down, but it did whet my appetite. There was a reason to think that we could make it all the way. My thinking was that I'd give it one more shot. My mindset was that 1969 would be it, my last shot at it.

TWENTY-TWO

THERE WAS SOMETHING else that happened in 1968 that changed things for me. I met Julie. I got introduced to her through football. Julie was a real pretty-looking woman, and I remember wondering why she was interested in me, me being a bit of a rebel and an outsider and what have you. But things got pretty serious between us pretty quickly.

Julie's father, Jim Mills, was on the committee at South Fremantle and he'd played for them years ago. Jim was a rough old diamond, and we finished up becoming really good friends, but at first he was dead against the relationship. He also had a couple of sons, who I got on with from the start, but Julie was his only daughter, and he was very protective. He was high up in the public service and he'd done a stint in Darwin at one point. He tried to stop Julie from going out with me. He put pressure on her and she had to leave home. She and a friend of hers got a flat.

Meeting up with Julie put an end to my annual spell in Darwin to play footy with the Buffaloes. We were planning to get married, and we were talking about starting a family, so naturally she didn't want me disappearing for months at a time and I couldn't argue with that.

We did get married, in 1969. I'd bought some land in Sorrento, thanks to my footy income. We built a brand-new house and moved out there, but it didn't really work out for us. In those days, Sorrento was like going to Yanchep; it was still all bush. Julie's family were all in Applecross, south of the river, and she said she felt so far away from them, up there on the northern fringes. So what I did was buy a place closer in. It was a swap in effect, exactly the same value as the Sorrento place.

So we moved into Townsend Road in Subiaco, right near the corner with Bagot Road. That made me smile, going from Bagot Road Darwin, to Bagot Road Subiaco. I went and stood underneath the road sign, got a photo and sent it back to Mum and the family.

WITH SUMMERS IN Darwin off the agenda, I was in Perth for the full pre-season for 1969. I wasn't too thrilled about that because Polly worked us hard. But we also got to know him better, and to understand what he was on about and his methods. We did a lot of socialising over that period, golf days and things like that. The team really moulded together as a unit.

And by our second year together, Polly and I had worked each other out pretty well and had a really good combination going in the ruck. Most weeks we would both start on the ball, and we would both play the majority of the game in the ruck. Pol would change to the forward pocket when he wanted a break – which wasn't that often – and I would rest in the back pocket. And that was just as well; if I'd been a forward pocket ruckman, I never would've got on the ball.

I remember a few years back walking into a function at the same time as Pol. It was for the 200 gamers club, at the dinner they have every year. As we walked in, there were Graham Moss and Ron Alexander yacking away to each other. Pretty good ruckmen, both of them. They see us walk in, and Graham Moss said, 'Well, here come the two dirtiest bastards I've ever played football against.'

I played innocent and looked over my shoulder, and said, 'Who are you talking about?'

'You and bloody Farmer!'

'You've got to be kidding. We both grew up in Christian homes.'

We all had a chuckle and got on with the business of the night. Me and Pol were no dirtier than anyone else. We were just better at it, more of the time.

Pol and I talked tactics a lot. After training, or at one of the pleasant Sunday mornings, or whenever the occasion arose, out of the blue he'd say, 'Come on Demo. I want to talk to you.' We experimented. Pol used to say, when this happens, we should do this. We worked our systems out.

It was a different world then to what you see today, with two blokes putting their hands up for permission to jump, and three field umpires watching them like hawks. We had one umpire, with his head down as he bounced the ball, and four ruckmen, two from each side, all milling around hoping to get first hand to the ball.

Our basic system for bouncedowns in the centre and around the ground wasn't that complicated. Generally he faced towards our goal, and I'd be on the other side. His instructions were that if the bounce was straight up or favoured him, it was his; if it favoured my side, it was mine. Whichever one of us wasn't going for the knock, it was our job to give the other feller a clear run. 'If it's mine, I want you to make sure that the bloke that's near me doesn't touch me.

And I'll do the same for you.' I'd pretend to be going for the ball but I'd take the other bloke out.

The same for boundary throw-ins. Sometimes you'd just have to go on your own. But the way we liked to play it, if we were both there for the throw-in, was for him to hang back while I took the front position. 'If it's possible,' he'd say, 'I don't want those blokes getting off the ground.' So I'd step on one bloke's foot, and hold the other bloke's shorts. Pol would go up and there'd be no one with him, because I'm hanging onto two blokes on the ground. He just flew up, grabbed the ball, and away we'd go. The other fellers'd be screaming at the umpires, but we never used to get caught, we'd always get away with it. We never used to argue; we'd just get on with the game.

And the thing is, whilst I joke about it, the toe-treading and the jumper-holding was not the main thing. The real art was actually in positioning and bodywork. Pol was the greatest body man I've ever seen, be it manoeuvring or climbing up on top of them. He'd put his knee in some bloke's hip and up he'd go. And it was always done within the rules of the game. I always used to chuckle when you'd see a big high ball come in. I always knew he was going to get it, no matter that it was two to one. He just used to manoeuvre them. All of a sudden, you'd see one bloke lurching over and one bloke going backwards, and *boom*, Polly's got the ball. I learnt so much about the art of bodywork just from watching him. You learn how to manoeuvre people without them even realising they're being manoeuvred.

After a full year playing with Pol in 1968, coming into that 1969 season, the two of us had things pretty well worked out between us, and we were just part of a team that was physically tough, mentally tough, and after the disappointment of '68, hungry.

TWENTY-THREE

MY RECOLLECTION OF that 1969 home and away season is that we started slowly, but that we came home absolutely flying. For three years running before that, Perth had beaten East Perth in the grand final. But that year, East Perth set the pace, and it was us and Perth chasing them, and jockeying with each other for second spot and the double chance.

East Perth had appointed Pol's old coach from the '50s, Jack Sheedy, as their coach. Their star player was Mal Brown. He won the Sandover that year and all of the media awards. He was only twenty-two but he'd been playing for years and he was good.

When Brown was in his prime, Pol would sometimes say, 'You're on Brownie. I don't care where he goes, back pocket, centre half-back, centre, you follow him. Only if he goes in the ruck can you stay in the ruck.'

I'd have a bit of a dig back, just for the sport of it, saying, 'Why don't you go on him for a change?'

'Because I'm the captain-coach, and I'm the boss. Just follow him.'

Now before I start talking about Brownie, there's a couple

of things I should say. The first is that in all the games of footy I played with West Perth and with the Buffaloes, I never once got reported. I played hard, but I played fair, and I was never a fighter or a brawler. My old mentor Froggie had drummed it into me. 'You can't do two things,' he said. 'You either play football, or you go and learn how to box. If you want to fight, you go in the ring. You want to play footy, you go out on an oval. You cannot mix the two.'

The second is that me and Brownie became good mates. We've done a lot of media together, and when he's in town, he sometimes comes to the weekly lunches I have with Johnny Miller the jockey, and some of my old footy mates. He's a good feller.

We became the best of mates, but when we were playing football, we weren't. On the field, he had the foulest mouth you've ever heard, and he used to like throwing his weight around. Every time I had a chance, I'd run through him. And vice versa – he'd have a go at me. Don't get me wrong. The man could play. He won a Sandover, and he deserved it, but Brownie had white-line fever. He was Doctor Jekyll and Mr Hyde. Him and I blued all the time.

There was an art to that physical side of the game, and as the years passed I learnt all about it – from what other players used to do to me when I was still learning the game. You'd be in a contest for the ball, and if you can get to it before him, it's yours. But some of them would hang back just a bit and wait for you to pick it up, and then go through and knee you in the head, or whatever. You learn not to be stupid. Sometimes you don't pick the ball up, you just keep running, straight at the bloke. I've hit him fair and square in the chest, and down he goes. I turn round and pick up the ball, and off we go. I used to do it all the time. And Brownie would do it to me if he got half a chance. But sometimes he'd cross the line of what was fair and square.

I'm not sure if it was that '69 season or not, but one time when we played at Perth Oval, which was their home ground, he had a go at me. I ducked, and he missed. 'You missed, you wanker,' I said. The trainers ran out and grabbed hold of me, because I was going to hook him. 'Don't hit him, don't hit him, he's already reported,' they were saying. And they were two East Perth trainers, not West Perth trainers! As you can tell from what I'm saying, Brownie had got me just a little bit riled up.

After the game, once I'd got dressed, I went and knocked on the door of their rooms. The doorman opened the door and I saw Brownie, and I said, 'Tell that big fat bastard over there to come outside. I want to talk to him.' *Bang*, he slammed the door. Five minutes later, two coppers came and escorted me off the ground. Me and my mate Brownie!

Thinking about it, that probably wasn't '69, unless he went to the tribunal and got off, cos you can't win the Sandover if you're suspended. Mind you, I've also seen reports that in our third game that year, he put Pol down behind play; so maybe it was.

Anyway, in '69 we played them three times in the home and away rounds, as per normal. And the results were one win each and a tie in that third game, so you could say there wasn't much between us. Coming into the finals, the bookies had East Perth as favourites, which was fair enough, because they'd finished two games clear in first place. But Pol always said the only point of the home and away season was to finish top two so that you got the double chance. Nothing else really mattered, you started square come finals time. And we snuck into second place ahead of Perth with wins in our last couple of games.

As it turned out, once we'd got there to the second semi, we didn't need the double chance. There's a lot of stories told about that game. They say the first quarter was one of the toughest ever seen. But to tell you the honest truth, it's not one of the games that has stayed in my memory. I can remember Bradley Smith from East Perth going through Brian Pleitner, and that it was on. But all I really know is that we won it, and we won it well. It had taken ten years and 190 games, but I was through to a grand final at last!

THE 1969 GRAND Final. It's hard to know where to start. I've had some good times in my life's journey, but that day, and the week either side of it, are pretty hard to beat.

There were two weeks between the second semi and the grand final, of course. There was no thought of slacking off or recovering in that first week; Pol kept training us hard and kept us on our toes. And somewhere in that first week, Les Day came to see me. Les was a committee man and the club secretary. Him and me had always got on, despite my blues with the club hierarchy.

He said the club wanted to bring my mother down to see the grand final and asked what I thought about that idea. I was blown away. I hadn't put the idea to them or put the thought in their head. Not as far as I can recall, in any way. And more than anything else in my time at West Perth, it made me realise that I was appreciated there and I was valued. Anyway, Les rang her up, and invited her down.

Convincing her to come was another thing though. It wasn't that she didn't want to, but she'd never been outside the Northern Territory except when she'd been evacuated to Victor Harbour with me in 1942, and she'd never been on an aeroplane and didn't like the thought of getting on one of those contraptions one little bit. She wanted to know why she couldn't catch the bus. She wanted to know where she was going to stay. One drama after another. But we got it sorted out.

I told her there wasn't enough time for the bus, it'd take a week, and the game'd be come and gone. I lined up some friends, Benny Lew Fatt and his wife Sandra, to organise her at that end, and get her onto the plane and sit with her. She was still a bit reluctant but they talked her into it. They promised to look after her and she stayed with them down here. She respected the fact that I had enough on my mind with the grand final coming up, and she was happy as Larry with Benny and Sandra. I saw her when she got in, made sure she was all set, and I did a couple of media things with her. But it was all business that week. We had a game to win.

I can still remember to this day the speech that Pol gave to us at the Thursday night players' tea two days out from the game. Not the words, but the feeling that it created in me. There was no clenched fist stuff. He was never one for shouting, or never one for being emotional with us guys. He just laid it on the table. This is what we've got to do, this is how we're going to do it. We owe it to all our people, all our supporters, and you owe it to yourselves. Quietly. Very quietly. We were all quiet too, just sitting there, just listening to him, mesmerised. It was just the most fantastic speech of inspiration I ever heard. We were ready to run through brick walls. I remember being a bit worried that we still had to wait through Friday and Saturday and hoping we didn't use up all our energy.

~

ON THE DAY, I didn't need any more speeches or anything like that. I was pumped. I just wanted to get out there and get on with it. When we ran out on the ground, I spotted Mum in the crowd. There was a big heap of Darwin people who had come down, and she was sitting with all of them behind the goal, with a West Perth band like a scarf. I knew that she was right. From there, it was down to business.

We were the physically stronger side and we were skilful. And we knew when to be physical and when to be skilful. We had them on the back foot from that second semi, and we pressed our advantage. That first quarter, we just blasted them off the park.

Once we got Mal Brown spitting and spewing he was gone, because he wanted to go and nail blokes. And while he's nailing a bloke, his man's up the other end kicking a goal. 'Thanks Mal, you beauty,' we'd stir him up a bit more.

We had it wrapped up by half-time. It was like a demolition, and the fact that it was East Perth made it even sweeter. It's a strange feeling being out there on the field in a grand final, still playing, still going as hard as you can, but knowing you've got it won.

I never relaxed until that final siren. I still find it hard to put into words what it really meant, winning that flag in '69. I think it was like a vindication. It made those ten years worthwhile. Not just all the games, and the thousands of hours on the training track, but also all the big decisions and commitments I'd made along the way to leave home and build myself a new life in Perth. And being the mature and responsible person that I am, when that siren blew, all those feelings translated in my mind to the thought that I'm going to get pissed for a week.

But before I could get down to the serious business of

celebrating the win, there was something else to cap it all off. I was voted the winner of the Simpson Medal as the best player on the ground in the grand final. It wasn't like these days where the medal winner gets called up on the podium before they present the premiership cup, but that didn't matter one little bit. What an honour!

There is no doubt about it, that 1969 grand final was the sweetest day of my football career. I've been lucky enough to win a few at West Perth and with the Buffaloes, but that flag is the one that means most to me. It was my first at the top level, and it was hard-won, ten years in the making. On top of that, I had the Simpson Medal. And on top of that, the best thing of all, my Mum was there to share the day with me.

WEST PERTH WERE lucky to get the double chance that year. With two rounds of the home and away season to go, they were two games and percentage behind second-placed Perth. But they won their last two, and Perth got beaten by bottom of the ladder Claremont in their final game, to let the Cardinals sneak past them. Farmer finished second to Mal Brown in the Sandover Medal and most of the media awards.

The *West Australian*'s football writer Geoff Christian described the second semi-final as 'one of the most memorable and talked about final-round games on record . . . because of the sheer ferocity of the first quarter.' East Perth were shell-shocked, and conceded the first five goals to West Perth, who went on to win by twenty-six points.

Dorothy's attendance was a major feature of the pre- and post-game coverage of the grand final, and

Bill certainly turned it on for her. The *Weekend News* reported that 'West Perth ruckman Bill Dempsey, who had his mother from Darwin watching him for the first time in a league match, turned in probably the greatest performance of his career. He was easily the best man on the ground and marked in dynamic fashion.'

Another of their reporters said, 'Bill Dempsey could not have turned in a better game taking countless overhead marks and using his kicks wisely.' The *Sunday Independent* described him as 'the rock on which East Perth were sinking.' The stats sheets show Dempsey as taking thirteen marks for the day, with nineteen kicks and four handballs.

Only a consolation goal to East Perth on the final siren prevented the winning margin for the Cardinals being the greatest ever in a WAFL grand final.

TWENTY-FOUR

THEY DID THE presentation of the Simpson Medal on the Channel 7 footy show on the Sunday morning. I was feeling a little bit dusty and Mum had had a good night too. The club said that Channel 7 wanted me to bring Mum in with me, because the story had got out by then about her coming down for the game. I told them that might be a bit hard because Mum wasn't too keen on all that publicity stuff. But they kept on about how keen the TV mob were.

So I said to Mum, 'We've got to go to this place and have some morning tea and talk to a few people.'

'What for?'

'They just want to talk to me about the game. They have it every Sunday, and I'm the special guest today. They want you to be there too. There'll be people asking questions Mum, but you'll be right.'

If I'd told her it was for the TV, she wouldn't've come. She didn't seem to be aware of the cameras. We were sitting in there talking away. I was doing most of the talking, but she was answering a few questions too, and then they presented me with the medal. It was Doc Simpson who the medal was named for, or one of his sons. Once the presentation had been done, I turned around – this was all still on camera – and handed it straight over to Mum. I said, 'Here, this is for you. You're my mother, and you deserve it.'

She had a look at it, said, 'Thanks son,' and then sat there very demurely while they said their thanks and wrapped up the segment.

They had a replay on the Sunday night. Everyone but her knew that she was on the TV. We were all sitting around at this place having drinks and eats, and they all said, 'Dorothy, you've got to come and see the TV, there's a show about the footy on.'

'What do I want to see that for?'

'You've got to come, come here and sit down, have a seat.'

And she sees herself on TV. She looked at me, and I thought she was going to get up and crack me.

'You tricked me.'

'No I didn't. You saw the TV cameras there.'

'I didn't know what they were there for.'

'It's too late. You can go home and tell all your friends you've been on the TV.'

That's just how we used to talk to each other. But she was very proud. She only stayed a couple more days before she flew home to Darwin and she took my Simpson Medal with her.

I'd lined up to get some time off work, so after I'd seen Mum off, the celebrations kept going. I think we partied for nearly two weeks. There were some real party boys in that team, and after the season and the success we'd had, we reckoned it was fair enough to let our hair down.

I'm not sure of the exact timeline, but not too long after the win, I managed to make my way up to Darwin for a visit. I didn't pull the boots on for the Buffaloes, '67–68 was my swansong with them. But all that mob were real proud of me. I felt humbled. And if there was any chance of me getting a big head, there was plenty up there knew how to bring me back down to earth. It was on that trip that I think Jimmy Anderson started with his line – that he kept up for ever afterwards, the cheeky so-and-so – about how I should be thanking him, that it was all down to him, that he was the one who deserved the credit for my whole career in Perth.

Mum had this group of friends, and they'd all play cards together and drink endless cups of tea. I was there at her place making the tea, and they were all asking about how her trip to Perth went.

'It was fantastic. I met all these wonderful people, and they looked after me. I've never been to a city before, and I was really happy. And Billy's team won the grand final, and that was good. And he won the Simpson Desert Medal.'

'Excuse me Mum – it's got nothing to do with the Simpson Desert.'

'Oh, shut your mouth,' she said, and carried on with her story.

As far as Mum was concerned, 'Simpson' meant the Simpson Desert and that was that. And my medal was the Simpson Desert Medal. So that's what it's been in our family, ever since.

THERE'S A SEQUEL to that story that I probably should tell now, before I get back to the chronological storyline.

Years later, I was back in Darwin again. A bunch of the family were sitting around, and I said, 'Mum, where's that Simpson Medal? I haven't seen it since the day I gave it to you in 1969.'

She got up and walked away.

My brothers were there, and my three sisters. 'What's wrong with her?' I asked.

'Don't ask.'

After Cyclone Tracy hit Darwin in 1974, she lost everything, including all my memorabilia that she was keeping for me. And that included the Simpson Medal. It just vanished, like so many other things, in the madness that was Cyclone Tracy.

That was the end of that, I thought. I got in touch with the Simpson family and explained what had happened. 'I just want to do a favour for my Mum. I'll pay for it, but I'd really like a replica of the medal.' They agreed, and got one made up for me, and I sent it up to Mum.

Then, a couple of years later, I'm sitting at home on a Saturday morning when I get a phone call.

'Bill Dempsey?'

'Yes, that's me.'

'It's Channel 10 in Adelaide here. We've got a bit of a surprise for you.'

And they told me this story about two prospectors from Andamooka. They were poking around looking for opals on the fringes of the Simpson Desert there, and they came across this funny-looking stone. They put it in their bag, and when they got back to their camp, they chipped off all the grit and stuff, and guess what? It's the Simpson medal!

I listened to this yarn, and I said, 'You're pissing on me.'

'No. It's the Simpson Medal, 1969, awarded to Bill Dempsey.'

'You're joking. You must be smoking opium.'

But it was.

I thought it was downright spooky. Twilight Zone stuff. My Simpson Desert Medal turning up in the Simpson Desert, found by a couple of opal prospectors. But Mum wasn't fazed at all when I told her, or surprised. Her theory was that all those willy willy winds – the devil devils, as she called them – took it down there.

TWENTY-FIVE

I MIGHT HAVE had family and friends always happy to bring me down to earth back in Darwin. Here in Perth the footy gods did much the same for West Perth, when 1970 rolled around.

It's a mystery to me what happened that year. We lost a couple of good players. John Wynne went to South Australia and Bill Valli to Victoria, but other than those two, we had virtually the same team. Maybe we were still celebrating from '69, maybe we were too relaxed. I could never put my finger on it, but we just never got going – the whole year was a fizzog.

There is one game I remember from that year though, and it wasn't a West Perth one, it was WA against Victoria at the MCG. I played fourteen games of interstate footy for WA, but I was a reluctant state man. After all, I wasn't a West Australian. I was a Territorian, and I felt it was wrong that I should take the place of a West Australian. My first couple of games I was proud but after that I started to think it wasn't fair. But there was something different about that game against the Vics in 1970.

Polly was appointed captain-coach of the WA side. WA had never beaten the Vics at the 'G, never even come close really, and had copped some big hidings. I'd been on the wrong end of a couple of them. I think Pol knew it would be his last state game, and by the time it came round, it was already looking like West Perth would miss the finals. One way or another, he put a big effort into it; the preparation and the game itself. And he put me into the side as one of his back-up ruckmen, with our East Perth mates, Brownie and Brad Smith.

We were up against a fair old foursome on the Vic side. John Nicholls, Len Thompson, Sam Newman and Gary Dempsey, if you don't mind. They could all play a bit. Pol made sure I was in the team because he knew he could rely on me to do my support act the same as I did for him at West Perth. We knew all one another's moves, how to help one another. And he could rely on me to step in front of fellers, or jump off their feet; use my body to clear a path for him so he could do his thing. The old code: as long as we're getting the ball, we're winning.

It was an absolute dog of a day; the 'G was just a mudheap. That was supposed to favour them – everyone reckoned the Sandgropers were no good on a wet track – but I reckon it just helped level things out, and we played out of our skins, with Pol leading the way. We matched them all day.

Coming into the last quarter we were only a goal down and we had all the play. Right through that last quarter we had the ball in our forward line. Pol's idea was to keep it locked in. It was too muddy for any finessing or pinpoint passes or anything like that. He reckoned eventually they would make a mistake and we'd get the goal that we needed, and then we'd run away with it. So he pulled the forward pocket ruckman out to form the arc.

The trouble was, that left Gary Dempsey on his own on

the full-back line. He must've taken fifteen marks in that game. Right through that last quarter, we kept kicking it in. He kept marking it and kicking it back. It was like kick-to-kick at training. Dempsey was laughing his head off. Me and Pol were arguing there on the half-forward line for the last fifteen minutes. I said to put him back, put our bloke back. At least he might punch a ball, get it on the ground. We might soccer a goal or something. Pol said, 'I'm the captain-coach, not you.'

We lost by five points.

We should've won that game. It would've been something, beating the Vics at the 'G.

AFTER THE GAME, the two teams were mingling and Gary Dempsey came up to me. I'd met him, but I didn't really know him that well.

'I want to buy you a drink, Bill.'

'You're the last bastard I want to have a drink with. We could've created history here today if it wasn't for you, you mongrel.'

'Yeah, but it was good fun.'

'You big long streak of pelican shit,' I told him.

Well, we got talking. He was a real nice bloke Gary, a gentleman. He asked me what I was doing that night, it seemed like he was up for kicking on. But I had to make my excuses. My younger brother Dennis was living in Melbourne at that time. He'd started off as a ringer on the stations round Katherine. Then he'd become a slaughterman, a meatworker. Started at Katherine, then Darwin, Wyndham, Broome, and somehow he'd finished up working at the meatworks there in Melbourne.

Dennis was a real good guitarist. Played lead guitar, did vocals. He had a country and western band; they played Merle Haggard and all that stuff. Anyway, Dennis's band were playing that night at some bloodhouse pub in Fitzroy. I'd promised to come and see them, and, of course, I wanted to catch up with Dennis anyway. So I explained all this to Gary, and said I'd have to make my excuses.

'Would it be all right if I come along?' he says.

I was a bit taken aback. 'I've got to tell you, there'll be mostly Aboriginal people there.'

'That's alright. I've got nothing against Aboriginal people.'

So off we went, me and Gary, the two Dempseys. We walk into the bar, and you wouldn't believe it! It's Victoria, see. Melbourne. They all just mobbed Gary Dempsey, they loved him. All these Aboriginal women hanging off him. None of them were taking any notice of me.

After a while, Dennis called the place to order from up on the stage. 'I know youse all know Gary Dempsey there. He just played a big game for Victoria in the interstate footy match today. But I've got to let you know that that feller there with him is Bill Dempsey. He played in that same game for Western Australia. And he's my brother.'

There was this big cheer. Gary was loving it. The place just went off. A great night!

THERE'D BEEN SOME talk that Polly would pull the pin at the end of 1970, but he signed up for one more year as our captain-coach. The big change to our team in '71 was that we managed to recruit Peter Steward from North Melbourne. I could never work out why they let him go. Peter was an absolute gun of a player at centre half-back. He was hard,

25th April 1975, Bill's 300th game *Courtesy of Westpix, WAN-0037101*

Coach Graham Campbell and captain Dempsey with the 1975 premiership cup
Courtesy of Westpix, TWA-0112393

Bill receives his MBE from Governor Sir Wallace Kyle
Courtesy of Westpix, TWA-0112394

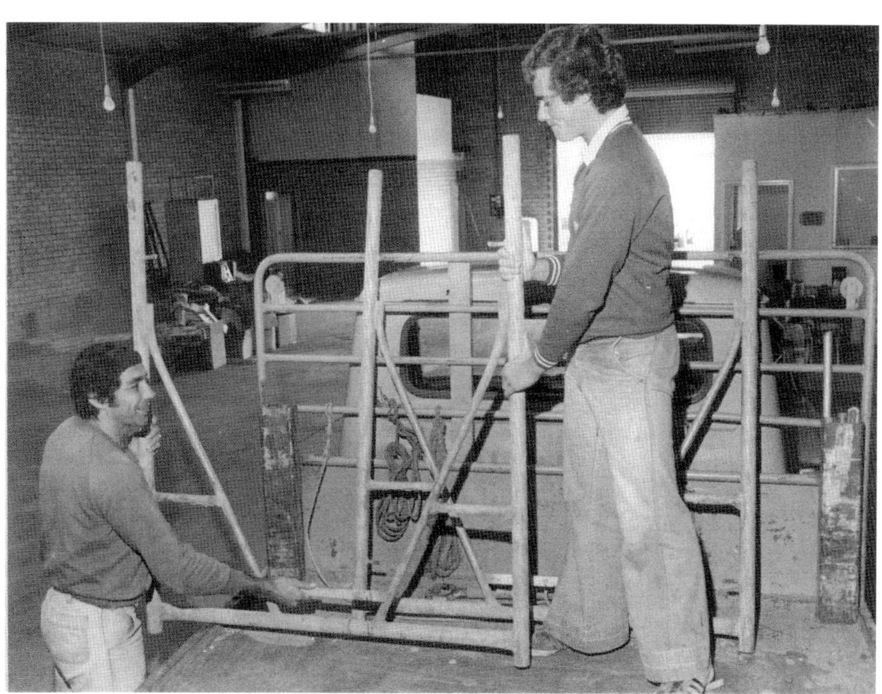

Bill and Barry Day loading scaffold at Dempsey Day Scaffolding, 1976
Courtesy of Westpix, TWA-0112396

Bill and Dorothy dancing *Personal collection*

Bill and Dorothy *Personal collection*

Bill and Jimmy Anderson *Personal collection*

Bill and friends in Darwin at his nephew Tony Curtis's home in the early 2000s.
L to r: John Clinch, Tony Curtis, Bill, Stan Hart, Trevor Schofield, Ron Biok
Personal collection

Bill and Mel Whinnen at the new Whinnen Dempsey Stand at Joondalup Oval in 1995
Courtesy of Westpix, TWA-0112397

Bill with his Simpson Medal *Courtesy of Westpix, TWA-0049691*

Jeran and Bill with Judy and Ken McAullay at the WA Football Hall of Fame induction dinner in 2019 *Courtesy of Westpix, TWA-0101313*

Bill Dempsey *Courtesy of Westpix, TWA-0054406*

cool under pressure, and he was the most powerful kick I've ever seen. And on top of that, he was a good bloke.

Pol had announced it would be his last year and there were all sorts of accolades for him. We all made a guard of honour for him when he ran out early in the season for the game where he broke Jack Sheedy's record for the most games by any player in the country. Not long after that, he brought up his 350th.

We still had a good side, but I think other sides had worked us out a bit more, and we seemed to struggle a lot through that season. It was a harder year than '69. On the ladder, the season rolled out a bit like the way '69 unfolded. East Perth were runaway leaders and we just snuck into second spot. Only that year, they beat us in all three home and away games.

In the finals, we did it the hard way, and also had a bit of luck. East Perth beat us in the second semi, and we only just scraped through the preliminary final. There was an East Fremantle player, Gary Fenner, who missed a shot just before the siren that would've put them in front. Coming into the grand final, East Perth were the red-hot favourites and we were the underdogs. That suited me. I always preferred to be the underdog because I think it made you fight harder.

Brownie had been made captain-coach of East Perth that year. In the lead-up to the game, he made a bit of a goose of himself talking about how they'd fight us on the field, fight us behind the grandstands and all this rubbish. But I don't think that made any difference to anything. Most of the public build-up was about it being Pol's last game.

Inside the club, we just went about the business. As far as I was concerned, it wasn't about Pol, and that certainly wasn't the message he gave us. People talk about his speech before the game as being the greatest thing they've ever heard. For me, the '69 one is the one that really stays in my head, but it was a top speech, in that firm, calm way of speaking he had. And it did the job; it got us up.

We didn't smash them the way we did in '69, but we were in front all day. We got the job done, and we had two flags in four years. Nothing could match the high of '69 for me, but it was sweet, and I suppose it underlined the fact that we really were a good team, that the first one wasn't just a flash in the pan.

Polly had announced his retirement but I did have a crack at talking him out of it. I said to him, 'You're still playing pretty good footy, and West Perth's still not a bad side – why are you giving it away?'

He said, 'Demo, I've been here four years; we've won two premierships. I don't want to wear out my welcome. I think it's time to move on.' He wanted to go out with a bit of pride, to prove to the knockers that he could still do it. It meant a great deal to him, that '71 premiership.

IT WAS AN honour to play with Pol for four years as his vice-captain and ruck partner. An honour and a pleasure. After all, we play this game with the aim of winning flags, and under him, we had a 50 per cent strike rate – two out of four. That's close to as good as it gets in the footy world.

Individually speaking, I probably hit my peak in 1966, the year I won the B&F at West Perth and all the media awards. But, even though it might be a cliché, it's true, those things aren't what you play the game for. You play for your club and its supporters, the fans that come and cheer you on every Saturday, come what may. You play for your mates and your team, and the feeling you get at the end of a winning game.

I'll take '69 and '71 over '66 any day of the week. And I thank Polly Farmer more than anyone else for making that possible.

I can say without hesitation that he was the best player that I saw, and the best that I played with or against. They broke the mould when they made Pol; he was one of a kind. Polly Farmer was just born to play footy. Even though I was a seasoned player when he came to West Perth, I think I learned more about footy and about the art of ruckwork from him than from anyone else over my career.

He liked to stir me up on the field because he seemed to think I played better angry. And I didn't mind having a crack back at him. A lot of the other guys were a bit in awe of Pol, which is understandable, but right from the start, I'd say to him, 'You can stand over these other fellers, but don't try it with me.' We blued all the time on the field. But we had a respect for each other. And we had a chemistry. And we had a shared attitude of doing what needed to be done, as long as it was to the advantage of our side, the Cardies. When it mattered, we had a common understanding.

As I said earlier, we remain, as far as I know, the only two Indigenous men to be the captain and vice-captain of a senior Aussie Rules footy team. We've been named as teammates in the West Perth team of the century and the AFL's official Indigenous team of the century.

We were a pair of mission boys. We both had nothing, and came from nowhere. We were about as different in character as you can get; oil and water, chalk and cheese, all those clichés. We were never going to be bosom buddies – Pol was never a drinker and smoker and all-round carouser like me – but we were always friends, and as the years passed, we always stayed in touch.

His kids were littlies when he came back west after his

stint in Geelong. I've known them just about all of their lives. Young Kim, in particular, has become a very good friend to me over the years, a bit like a favourite niece. She has played a big part in prodding me along to get this story down, and in helping to make it happen.

It was terribly sad to witness the last years of Pol's life as the Alzheimer's got hold of him. And even more shocking to find out just recently that it was the concussions from his footy career that were the real problem.

To be given the privilege of being a pallbearer at his funeral in 2019 was a very proud and a very sad day.

TWENTY-SIX

THERE WAS SOMETHING else that happened around then that was pretty important in the way my life panned out. I've just been waxing lyrical about Pol and 1971 and the second flag and so forth. But as I remember, at the start of the '71 season, I wasn't quite so upbeat. '70 had been a fizzog, and I started the year a bit out of sorts, with thoughts about giving it up running through my mind.

I was still pretty much a newlywed. Julie and I were trying to start a family. I had a second income coming in from footy. But I was still in the accounts department at Humes. I'd never seen footy as the be-all and end-all in life. I'd always had thoughts of trying to better my situation. I'd used the Victorian bait to improve my bargaining position with the club, and in their minds, that possibility was still in the air, but that wouldn't work forever for me. I was looking for a way to set me and my family up for a better future. I haven't got the records or the details to be dead sure, but I think it was in 1971 that this unfolded.

There were a few people within the club who were aware of my thinking. Lizard Porter, who'd taken me under his wing in the early days, had got onto the committee, and I'd always got on well with Les Day, who was on the committee too. And there was a feller called Frank Margaria who'd played for West Perth. He was in the building game. They must've all talked amongst themselves. Next thing, I get called into a committee meeting.

'We want to put a proposal to you, Bill.'

'Oh yes. I'm all ears.'

'We want to know if you're interested in starting up a business.'

'What sort of business?'

'Scaffolding. Do you know anything about scaffolding?'

'No, but I could learn.'

It was a two-pronged thing from their point of view, I suppose. I'd given the club bloody good service by that time. Eleven years and over 200 games. And there was certainly at least some of those blokes on the committee, maybe all of them, who genuinely wanted to help me out and see me do well. But if it panned out, it would also be a way of tying me in to the club for the rest of my playing days, because the proposal and the club were bound up together.

I didn't want to seem to be too enthusiastic or anything like that. I was trying to be Mr Cool. But I asked them how it would all work. They said they would organise finance and premises, and line up some initial clients, and from there, it would be up to me.

I was keen. I'd always wanted to be in charge of my own destiny, to do something for myself rather than just work for other people. And this seemed to be my chance.

I went to see one of my oldest mates, Maxie Cummings. Maxie was a Retta Dixon boy like me, but he'd also spent a big chunk of his mission time out at Croker Island. He was a cheeky bloke and Croker was where they sent the ones they regarded as troublemakers. Maxie had come down to Perth not that long after me. He more or less followed me down, I suppose, not for football, just looking for work. He was a labourer and a truck driver Maxie – a real good worker.

We went down the pub and I said, 'Listen, you and I have got to sort out this scaffold company.'

'What scaffold company?'

'We're going to start one.'

'We know bugger all about bloody scaffolding.'

'I know we know nothing but we've got to learn. I'll do all the office work, and you've got to be the truck driver. That's how we'll start.'

'Am I going to get paid?'

'We'll sort that out, but I need you to come and support me.'

Maxie agreed, and I went and told West Perth I'd give it a go.

Les Day was the one who'd put the idea together and done all the planning. Him and me went half and half, and set up Dempsey Day Scaffolding. Les organised the land for our premises, a yard on Frobisher Road in Osborne Park, and the finance to get us started, but all of the operations and management were down to me.

IT'S CHANGED A lot since the '70s, but the basics of the business were pretty straightforward. You needed a truck, the actual scaffold, which was made up into what we called frames, and the karri planks, always fourteen feet long, to lay on the frames. Each layer of frames was called a lift. Each lift was five feet high, so the brickies could lay five feet of bricks, and then we'd add the next lift, they'd lay another five feet, and so forth. We would supply and erect the scaffold, putting each new lift up when they were ready for it, and then take it all down in one go when that job was finished.

You had to know what you were doing, which we quickly got on top of. I went to scaffold school and got my scaffolder's licence. You had to be reliable, and be able to get on with the builders and the other contractors. The real art to it though, was in putting in your quote for a job. You had to be low enough to beat the competition, but not so low as you'd lose money on the job. And I found that I had a knack for that side of it.

I got it down to a tee I was a bit of a mathematician. I designed the costing structure, and I had it like a graph. I could go to a job and take the measurements, and I'd go *zip*, multiply it with this, this and this, and *bang*, there's your price. I could give a price within half an hour, and most times, we got it right.

Our first jobs came through that West Perth network, Frank Margaria and his builder mates, and other members at West Perth who were in the building game. And that continued to be a good source of work for us, but I built it up well beyond that.

At first it was just me and Maxie, and we had a bloke round the corner manufacturing the frames for us. Then we put on a guy by the name of Remo Raymond. He was a Torres Strait Islander who'd come to Perth to play rugby. He was a qualified welder, so he started making up the frames for us in-house. We got more clients and so we needed more frames. Then we got a second truck and put a few more guys on. None of this happened overnight, of course. We grew slowly, bit by bit, which was good.

Les did the company accounts, but I handled all the wages

books, as well as the quoting and general administration, plus I was giving Maxie and the boys a hand on the sites. We had all sorts working for us. All fit young blokes. Some of them were footy players. We had a Japanese, we had a Samoan, two blackfellers, three white men. We were like the United Nations. And it was hard work. Those fourteen-foot karri planks took a bit of lifting. That was good for me, because it kept me fit. I was as strong as a bloody bull.

So, from '71 on, if that's the year we started, I was a business owner and manager as well as a footballer. It kept me busy, let me tell you.

TWENTY-SEVEN

POLLY DIDN'T LISTEN to me, which was probably very wise of him, and retired at the end of the 1971 season. So West Perth went with the succession plan they had set in place the year before and appointed Peter Steward as the captain-coach. That was always the idea when they recruited him, that he would step into Pol's shoes, and that's a tall order for anyone.

As I said, Peter was a gun player, and a top bloke, but the truth is, he was just one of the guys; he never really wanted to be a coach. The club had helped set him up in a bottle shop business when they brought him over, and he would've been happy to concentrate on that and playing, but he did the right thing by them and took the job on.

We were alright, but I think it was inevitable that we were going to slip back a bit after two flags in three years and Pol's departure. We went at about half and half and finished fourth, and then we got knocked out in the first semi by Perth. Peter stepped down as the coach and as captain after that year but stayed on with the club as a player.

So coming into 1973, the club needed a new captain, and it really came down to a matter of whether it was going to be me or Whinney, as the two senior players. I think most of the hierarchy in the committee wanted to give it to Mel, but there was a bit of a ruffle by all the people underneath. I believe there were even some who said, 'If Bill Dempsey isn't made captain, we're going to leave the club.' It's not that anyone had anything against Whinney at all, but Mel was a very quiet, unassuming sort of a guy. I think I was seen by a lot of people as more outspoken – a bit of a loudmouth, if you like – and more of a natural leader. The way I put it is that I didn't take any shit from anyone. People knew that, and seemed to think that would be the right sort of attitude for the captain of the club.

So I was offered the captaincy and I accepted it with absolute pride. I'd come a fair way from being a mission boy on Bagot Road in Darwin.

The only trouble was that we also needed a new coach. The club went for the standard formula for the WAFL clubs in those days; go find a Victorian. The one they found was a feller called Dennis Jones. He'd played for Melbourne in the early '60s when they were a gun side, without ever being a star. Pol had come across him. I remember bumping into him at one point and him asking what I thought about Dennis. I could tell from the way he asked it and the look on his face that he didn't rate the feller very highly.

I don't like to speak ill of anyone, but I've got to be honest, I can't find a lot good to say about Dennis as a coach. I never got on well with him at all. He was a bit of an arrogant Victorian. He'd say things like, 'You guys wouldn't get a game in the seconds back in Victoria.'

One time at training when he first started, he said, 'I'll show you guys how to do bodywork.' He asked who was the best drop-punt kick, and the boys said Normy Knell. And he asked who was the best mark, and they said me. He sent Normy off forty yards or so, and said, 'Come with me, and I'll show the boys how to do bodywork against supposedly good markers.' Well, I was taking one-handers, behind him, in front of him, on the side, everything. He tried to humiliate me but it worked in reverse.

And for some reason, he seemed to have it in his mind to make it hard for Mel Whinnen and me, as the two oldest players. He did his best to make it difficult for us. Don't ask me why – some idea of discipline or setting an example or something.

Nevertheless, to give him his credit, he did get us playing okay that first year. We finished second on the ladder, and we actually won the second semi against Subiaco. But then we lost our full-forward, Phil Smith. Phil was worth five goals a game to us. And Subi knocked us over in the grand final. I busted my arse on the field for the whole year, as per usual, especially with the added responsibility as the captain, but there wasn't that good feeling about the place that you want in a footy club.

I'LL TELL YOU what was a good feeling that year, though. My son was born. Joshua.

Julie and I had wanted kids from the get-go, but as is the way with these things, it doesn't always happen straight away. Late in 1972 though, Julie got pregnant. It wasn't all smooth sailing. A couple of months before she was due, we were in a car accident, and Julie broke her ankle. It also turned the baby, so he was breech.

Poor Julie's there with her leg in plaster, and seven months pregnant. They didn't take the plaster off until the day that

Josh was born. I was lucky that I had Dempsey Day. I still had to keep it all going, but I had flexibility, so I spent a lot of time at home looking after her.

Josh was born on a Saturday at St John of God hospital in Subiaco. We played Subiaco at Subi Oval that day. As soon as the game was finished, I went straight to the hospital. He hadn't been born yet when I got there, but they told me I had to wait outside. I was thinking something must be wrong, because he was breech, you see. But it all turned out okay. Josh was born healthy, and I had a son!

I still had to be around at home because Julie could hardly do anything. So for at least six months, I took lots of time off, juggling the work stuff any way I could, until Julie got strong enough to do it. It was good really, because it bound us together as a family.

Me and Mum had always had a difficult sort of relationship, for the reasons I've explained. But little Josh was the apple of her eye. She worshipped the ground he walked on!

I HAD A lot on my plate coming into 1974. The business was growing and keeping me really busy, and I had a baby son at home. All my life, footy had been a pleasure and a release from the pressures of everyday life but that year was different.

1974 is the only season that I ever played in which my team won the wooden spoon. And I was the captain. We go from a grand final playoff to stone motherless last!

The wheels just fell off. It was not a happy team No one was happy. Least of all me, and I was the captain.

I remember one day that year, out at Bassendean, playing Swan Districts. We were getting belted. Max George, the

Swans full-forward, kicked fourteen goals. Just before half-time, the runner came out. He was a mate of mine, name of Ken Ferguson. He says to Whinney, 'The coach says you've got to come off the ground.' This was before the days of interchange, remember, once you were off, you were off for the rest of the game. And this was only a couple of minutes before half-time. He was trying to humiliate Mel.

I said, 'Whinney, don't go. You stay here.' I said to Fergie, 'Piss off, and go and tell that big fat bastard to go and get stuffed.'

When we got in at half-time, Fergie said he didn't have to take my message back – the whole oval had heard it.

So when we got into the rooms, you could've heard a pin drop. We're all sitting with our heads down, embarrassed because we're getting flogged. Dennis said to the president, Len Roper, 'Len, am I the coach of this football club?'

'Yes, Dennis, you are.'

'Well, I sent the runner out with a message to get a certain player off the field, and the runner was told to piss off.'

By this time, I'd had enough. I got up. I said, 'Dennis, the bloke's name is Mel Whinnen. You should not be in the same room as him. So why don't you piss off.'

He looks at Len. 'Can he talk to me like that?'

I looked at Len and the committee. 'Read my lips. Anyone wants to have a go at me – I'm ready for you. He is useless as rocking-horse shit.'

This is at half-time in the game. Nothing happened. Nobody said a word.

I looked at Dennis and said again, 'You shouldn't be in the same room as him.' [In the second half of that game, Round 13 of 1974, Swan Districts kicked 16 goals to 6, to run away to an 87 point win.]

Mel being Mel, he would never have said anything. He would've taken his medicine and gone off. But the way I saw it, being the captain, it was my job to stick up for the players. I said the things I said in the heat of the moment, but I didn't only do it in defence of Mel, or out of spite for Dennis. It was about who we were as a team and as a club. I wasn't going to see our champion player humiliated in that way.

Would you believe that at the end of that year Dennis came in to see me at work, in my office there in Osborne Park at Dempsey Day. He said, 'I'm going to put in for an extension. Would you support me as the coach?'

'You've got to be joking. You're asking the wrong bloke,' I said. 'I'm not going to support you.'

They didn't give the job to Jonesy. He was gone.

TWENTY-EIGHT

FOOTY-WISE, IT HAD been a pretty topsy-turvy few years. Flags in '69 and '71, a grand final in '73, and in between a sixth place, a first semi loss and a wooden spoon.

I was coming up for my sixteenth season. Whinney had played his 300th in the last game of '74, and I was sitting on 296. I didn't have much of a leap left in me anymore. I had to use my noggin and my bodywork to compete at the bounces and throw-ins or to take a mark.

But what was really burning in me was making up for the debacle of '74. We had virtually the same side still. I said to the players, 'Look, we have to bust our arses for this club. How embarrassing was that, coming last? What do you guys think about that? I reckon it's terrible. We've let all our members down, and we'll let them down again if we play the same sort of rubbish football.'

The club had gone down the same path of recruiting another Victorian. The bloke they got in was Graham Campbell, who'd played for Fitzroy. He was even less of a name in the footy world than Dennis Jones had been. I'm not running him down, but Graham was no coaching genius. He was a good bloke, though. He didn't think that Victoria was the only place on earth that could produce good players or good ideas, and he could stimulate the players, he respected them. He walked in, and he said, 'What a beautiful team I've got.' He changed the atmosphere around the place. But really, what we achieved was player-led. I, as the captain, and the rest of the team were determined to atone for the year before. We were humming.

I clocked up my 300th in the fourth round, and to tell you the truth, I don't remember a thing about it. Whinney and I played every game that year; he kept his four-game edge on me. And the team just rolled along. We played well, finished on top, and got the double chance.

What can I say about those two finals? Last year's wooden spooners won the second semi by more than ten goals and the grand final by over one hundred points! It was like living a fairytale. The '69 flag is still the one that holds a special place in my heart, but I can't tell you just how chuffed I was to be the captain of a West Perth premiership side and to hold up that cup. I felt like I'd reached the top of the mountain.

IT HAD A bit of a feel of a Buffaloes v St Mary's game, that '75 grand final. We had myself and Lindsay McGuinness and Leon O'Dwyer. I'd actually played with Lindsay's dad, Vincent, in my early years with the Buffaloes; he was from that same famous family of Buffalo players and activists that Steve Abala came from. Leon had played footy in the Territory with the Buffs before he came to West Perth. And by then, South Fremantle had their connection with St Mary's up and running. Seb Rioli was the first one to come down, in 1972, and through him, they got a mortgage on all the St Mary's boys. In '75, his brother Maurice joined him and so did Basil Campbell. Basil was actually a cousin of mine, through my Alice Springs family, not that that counted for much on the day.

I reckon that period there around the mid-'70s was when things started to change a bit, and the platform was laid for what we are seeing today, with Indigenous players becoming so important to the game, and a part of every club now.

We'd gone from the five on the lists when I started – me and Pol and Square Kilmurray, and Irwin Lewis and Des Davis – back to virtually just me. Syd Jackson had come and gone, over to Carlton. Keith Narkle started at Swans in '71 I think it was. John McGuire had started with East Perth in '73. He won a flag with them in '78 but he was always a cricketer more than a footballer – it was a crime that he never got picked for the state cricket team. I'm sorry if there's anyone I'm forgetting, but that was about it until the mid-'70s.

I like to think that us Territory boys had a bit to do with it starting to change. We mixed with all the local Noongars, and they saw it could be done, and slowly, slowly, the barriers started to break down. Stephen Michael came to South Fremantle. He was in that '75 grand final too, early in his career. What a player he was.

I'm not saying that everything was rosy all of a sudden. I still heard and saw some shocking things on the field and in the years after I retired. Coaches saying the most awful things to their Indigenous players. Abuse on the field, and from the crowds. It wasn't until years later when first Nicky Winmar, and then Michael Long, did what they did, that the game really started to come to grips with the issues. But I do believe that the tide started to turn towards the end of my career. And since I retired, it has been an absolute pleasure to watch that tide getting bigger and stronger every year.

I've had a few gongs and nominations come my way in the years since I retired. I can hardly keep track of how many different 'best of' type teams they put me in. But the one that I'm really proud of is being named in the AFL's Indigenous Team of the Century that they announced in 2005. They named me in the back pocket, alongside another Territory boy, Darryl White, at full-back. Polly was the captain and first ruck, of course. There were a couple of others of my vintage too: David Kantilla, and the one that really pleased me, Ted Kilmurray. They both got named on the interchange bench.

IT'S A FUNNY thing, you know. Over the years I managed to get it into my mind that the 1975 grand final was my last game, and the perfect ending. It's only as I've started to go back over it all that I've been reminded that I did go on for one more year. That shows how much I remember of the '76 season.

What did happen that year was that Mel Whinnen and I got awarded MBEs – Members of the British Empire. It still sounds strange in my ears today.

The nomination and the push for it came from people inside West Perth. They made a bit out of the fact that there'd never been two players at the same club at the same time with 300 plus games under their belts.

I got a letter from the Governor, saying that I'd been recommended for the MBE and that I had three months to think about whether I wanted to accept it or not. I realised it was a big deal. Pol had got one at the start of 1971 in the New Year's honours list. Apart from him, I think there was only one or two other footballers who had ever got one. But

I was never really a Queen and Country and Empire sort of feller. I wrote back to them and said, 'Thanks for the recognition, but, no, I don't want it. I don't want to accept it.'

The next thing I know, I get a phone call from my mother. 'Who the hell do you think you are?' she said to me.

'What do you mean?'

'I just had a phone call from the president of the West Perth Football Club, and he told me that the club recommended you and Mel Whinnen to get MBEs.'

'Yes. So what?'

'And you knocked it back?!'

'I'm a grown man. I can do what I like.'

'No you can't!'

She gave me what for. She reckoned it was about more than my ego and my feelings. 'That medal, that recognition, belongs to our family. It belongs to Retta Dixon Home where you grew up. It belongs to the Buffaloes. And it belongs to the Aboriginal people. You go and get it!'

So, of course, I did. Me and Whinney got dressed up like bloody wankers and went to Government House and got our gongs.

The first chance I got, I took it home to Darwin and gave it to her. I think it helped make up for the Simpson Medal and all the other memorabilia that had got blown away a couple of years earlier in Cyclone Tracy.

But didn't I get grief from Jimmy Anderson and the boys when I took it back there!

'What do you call that thing?' he reckoned.

'An MBE.'

'Gee, those white people are stupid.'

'What are you talking about, Jimmy?'

'What do they want to give you a medal for? An MBE?

You're already a Member of the Black Empire.'

'Piss off, Jimmy.'

I felt a bit embarrassed about the whole thing. But in the end, I finished up thinking Mum was right and I was sort of proud.

AS FOR THE footy that year, the team did okay. We made fourth place, and then got knocked out in the first semi by Perth. That was my last game of footy. My old mate Whinney went round for one more year but I was more than ready to hang up the boots by then. Seventeen years and 343 games with the Cardies. The two full seasons with the Buffs before I came down, and all those years in the '60s when I played in both competitions.

It was a fair old innings!

I managed to win three flags with each of my clubs, six in all. That was six pretty good end-of-season shindigs. For the last one, I'd accepted the cup as the captain of the premiership team there on Subiaco Oval. I'd had the privilege for four years of being the vice-captain and the ruck partner of the greatest player the game has seen.

It was beyond the wildest dreams of that seventeen-year-old boy in his first pair of long pants who jumped on a Fokker plane at Darwin airport with Jimmy Anderson in 1960.

My old mentor Froggie Snape and all my Buffaloes mates were proud of what I'd done.

Grandpa George had passed by that time, but sometimes when I looked in the mirror, I'd remember what he'd told me, and liked to think he was smiling down on me.

And while my dear old Mum would never say a good word to me to my face, my brothers and sisters would tell me about how proud she was of me, and how she boasted about me and stuck up for me. After all, I was a Member of the Black Empire with a Simpson Desert Medal. In some ways, we never got over the terrible start that was inflicted on us by the authorities of the time, but in other ways, we were as close as a mother and son can be. The family tell me that when I used to head back to Perth, she'd go into her bedroom and cry for me. I knew that she loved me but she kept it to herself.

I'd done what Jimmy the King demanded of me when he took off and left me there all on my own in Perth. I showed them that a Darwin boy, a Retta Dixon boy, could make it in the big time.

I might have hated training but I loved playing footy. I loved being a part of two big families at the Buffaloes and the Cardies. Not just the teammates and the friends I made amongst them, the friends for life. But that whole community of families and fans that make up the world of footy.

At one level, you'd like to keep going forever. But by the end of '76 I knew I'd reached the end of the road. The body was buggered. I wished Whinney luck for next season, and pulled the pin. It was time to get on with the rest of my life.

TWENTY-NINE

BILL DEMPSEY PLAYED seventeen seasons for West Perth, from 1960 to 1976. He was their captain for the last four years of this career. He played a total of 343 club games, second only to Mel Whinnen, who continued on in 1977 and got his tally to 371. No one stands higher in the West Perth pantheon than these two, the Cardinal Twins.

His value as a consistent player of the highest quality is perhaps best demonstrated by his performances in the Breckler Medal, the annual West Perth Best and Fairest count. After his first two seasons in which he was spending periods in the reserves, and establishing himself in the side, only once in fifteen years – the horror year of 1974 – did he finish outside the top six in the Breckler count.

He only took out the medal once, in 1966, when he was at the absolute peak of his powers and won a swag of the media awards. Other than that, Whinnen had a virtual lock on first place, with Bill having five runner-up finishes.

He played in an era of great ruckmen, matching

himself against the likes of John Nicholls, Len Thompson and Gary Dempsey in interstate games, and Jack Clarke, Graham Moss, John McIntosh and his mate Paddy Astone amongst others in the WAFL, and held his own against all of them.

Such things are a matter of debate and opinion, but there is a strong argument to be put that his four-year stint with Polly Farmer as the first ruck pairing for West Perth was possibly the best ruck partnership the game has seen.

Bill has already mentioned that he was named in the AFL's official Indigenous Team of the Century in 2005. He was also in the teams of the century of West Perth and the Northern Territory AFL, and is a designated AFLNT Hall of Fame Legend and an inaugural inductee of the WA Football Hall of Fame.

IN THE LISTS that are compiled of the most games played, the runaway leader is Craig Bradley of Port Adelaide and Carlton. With interstate matches, state of origin games and international rules matches against Ireland all included his tally is 501, well ahead of Peter Carey who played 467 games for Glenelg and South Australia. With fourteen state matches added to his West Perth games, Bill sits forty-first on this list at 357 games, equal with Matthew Pavlich.

There are no accurate records of games played in the Northern Territory league, and it might perhaps be a stretch to describe the NT competition as an equivalent to the AFL and the South and West Australian leagues. But let's make that stretch for the sake of argument. Bill himself certainly valued his games for the Buffaloes just as highly as his WAFL games.

Bill played two full seasons for the Buffaloes in the 1958/59 and 1959/60 seasons before he went to Perth. And he played for them from 1962/63 to 1967/68 during the WAFL off-season. Football historians in the Territory estimate that he played 'about 100 games' for the Buffaloes. Bill reckons it might have been closer to the 150 mark than the 100.

If these games were added to his official tally of 357, at the very least he would sit a very close third on the all-time list, just behind Peter Carey. Most probably he would be placed not far behind Bradley's 501, with the second highest number of games of senior football played by an Aussie Rules player.

THIS CHAPTER HAS already broken from the mould of the rest of the book, which is Bill's story, told in his own voice. Please forgive a further sidetrack from his collaborator.

Spending many dozens of hours listening to Bill's stories has been an honour and a privilege and a pleasure. But one aspect of it was very frustrating. I could never get him to talk seriously about himself as a footballer. Bill played his footy by the Buffaloes code that Froggie Snape and others instilled in him.

'When you pull the guernsey on, you bust your arse for that guernsey, and the team, and the supporters. You represent all these people, your family, your supporters, the whole lot. So you do your best. That's what I was taught.'

His approach to footy was never analytical. He was never going to be a coach. He did do a short stint coaching the West Perth reserves but threw it in at the end of the season 'because I got too emotional'.

And he has a determined, unshakeable modesty when it comes to talking about his own role in the teams he played in. He sucked me in. For a long time, I had Bill Dempsey down as a very good journeyman player, who achieved fame and admiration through his longevity in the game more than anything else.

I once compared him to Michael Tuck, the Hawthorn player and captain who for many years held the AFL games record. No one challenges Tuck's place as a great of the game, but nor does anyone rate him amongst the truly great players.

But when I started to talk to contemporaries who played with Bill and against him, I was pulled up on this, and it gradually became clear to me that I had under-rated him.

Bill Dempsey was a seriously good footballer.

But he won't talk about that.

So after a couple of arguments with him, I finished up saying that we are going to have to ask a few other people to speak for you.

So in the rest of this chapter, you will hear from some fellow players and commentators who were close observers of Bill Dempsey the footballer.

Steve Hawke

DENNIS COMETTI:
My uncle used to work with Bill Dempsey in the early '60s' at Humes in Subiaco. They were good friends. By the time I got to West Perth in 1967, Bill was an established star and because of that friendship, I always felt he took more than a casual interest in my progress. My father was a West Perth supporter; we lived about ten minutes from Leederville Oval, so fair to say, growing up, I saw a lot of the Cardinals and Bill. He was a remarkable player who, like many of the game's best, masked his courage behind an assortment of breath-taking skills. Bill wasn't big for the ruckman he was asked to be, but his leap was prodigious, his judgement uncanny and, for his size, he had agility second to none. I find it slightly odd that when I look back over my time in and around football, two of the best half-dozen marking players I've ever seen both happen to be called Dempsey. Not a common name but fair to say, it fits neatly, simply because both Gary and Bill shared uncommon brilliance overhead.

One of the most vivid memories from my playing days at West Perth is a game against East Perth in 1968. In my mind's eye, I can still see Bill with his head down trying to finesse his way through a pack while at the same time keep the ball in bounds, when a wild, reckless attempt to soccer almost connected his head. I was only a couple of metres away and saw firsthand where Bill drew the line. In a flash, he was nose to nose with Malcolm Brown, a man as erratic as he was big and powerful. Despite his quick move, Bill's demeanour was calm, a calmness that gently morphed into an exasperated smile with the words, 'I thought I recognised the boot.'

That story is not only true but serves to illustrate that brilliant players rarely get enough credit for their courage.

Bill falls into that category. He was fearless yet fair to a fault. He relished the contest and the result in equal measure. And while it might be just the romantic in me, I always felt Bill was acutely aware of who he represented beyond West Perth. He once told me that in his very early days he would often finish a reserves game at Leederville Oval before skipping across town to Perth Oval to watch two great Indigenous players, Graham Farmer and Ted Kilmurray, play for arch-rivals East Perth. Both won Sandover Medals and both were constant and tangible reminders to Bill of what was possible. No doubt he drew inspiration from the pair. Fitting then, that when all is said and done, all three can be mentioned in the same breath.

GEOFF CHRISTIAN:

Geoff Christian was regarded as the doyen of football writers in Western Australia. He began with The West Australian *in 1954 and was their senior football writer for over twenty-five years from 1961. No one was better placed to analyse and compare Dempsey the footballer. This extract comes from an article he wrote on 23rd April 1975 to mark the occasion of Bill's 300th game under the headline* The Legend of a Dempsey Named Bill.

Bill Dempsey, the boy from Darwin who became a man of distinction in Perth, will play his 300th league football match on Anzac Day for West Perth – the club that became his home in 1960 and his headquarters for success.

Dempsey, whose fifteen-year trek along the hazardous football trail has led him into football's hall of fame, will play his historic game against Subiaco at Subiaco Oval.

His name goes into the record book alongside those of Graham Farmer, Jack Sheedy and his football twin, Mel

Whinnen, as the only West Australians who have played in 300 league games.

Dempsey has long walked tall amongst WA's football greats, having kept in tune with his superb marking skills, his subtle use of timing at the hit-outs and his mastery of the oft ignored art of the tackle.

The Dempsey marking technique is unique. He makes hard marks look simple, his long arms stretch to places that rivals think they have covered, and the one-handed mark is part of his aerial acrobatics.

Those two wonderful one-handed marks in rapid succession in the 1973 second semi-final against Subiaco bear adequate testimony to Dempsey's superb reflexes.

When it comes to ruckwork, he is not endowed with great height. At 1.88m (6ft 2in) he is on the short side of some of his great rivals.

But what Dempsey lacks in inches, he more than makes up for in his sense of timing and the expert use of his body in the struggle for the hit-out.

The influence of Farmer, football's greatest ruckman, is evident in the Dempsey touch at the bouncedowns and throw-ins.

Farmer was Dempsey's coach between 1968 and 1971 and they formed one of the most formidable ruck batteries assembled in Perth.

Dempsey perfected a Farmer ploy of taking off early for the hit-outs. This technique enables him to leap slightly before his rival and come down early but with his body between his rival and the ball.

It is a frustratingly effective manoeuvre, specially useful in battle against the tall followers who have sprung up in football during the past ten years.

Few players are remembered for their ability to tackle, but in this case, only a gentle reminder is needed to bring back memories of the Dempsey tackle.

It was more spectacular a few years back when, as a lighter player, Dempsey used his agility and long arms to trap opponents, and it formed a vital part of his football make-up.

Football gave Dempsey his chance in life. Many others have had this chance and spoilt it, but it is a measure of this man that he has gone from strength to strength.

He has hardly put a foot wrong in his climb up the ladder of success. His rise from obscurity has been achieved with a minimum of fuss and a maximum of effectiveness.

Dempsey is a tough but fair competitor. Footballers do not play in the ruck for 300 games and not learn the art of self-protection.

But in these games, Dempsey has never been reported – a record of discipline that is hard to match by ruckmen who are involved in the game's hardest and most consistent clashes.

So Dempsey, the lad who came to Perth for only two years, stayed to become a football hero, and an example to all sportsmen.

MAL BROWN:

When I think of Bill Dempsey as a footballer, the phrase that comes to mind is, 'Upon this rock, I build my church.' That's the coach in me speaking I suppose, even though I never coached Bill. But he was one of those players you could build a team around.

He had a lot of different attributes as a player.

Above all, he was a beautiful mark. He had magnificent hands. In Victoria, Gary Dempsey from the Bulldogs used to sit in the backline and take those big marks. Well, that was Bill Dempsey in the WAFL. If people had the statistics of marks taken over the course of a career, Bill Dempsey would be right up at the top level.

He was a good kick. He could run all day but he never looked like he was getting past half-pace. He was one of those blokes that just floated, drifted around the ground. As a player, he was just so cool. He always had time and he never seemed to panic and he never rushed. He was just a very, very steadying influence. I say this as an opponent and as someone who played thirteen or fourteen state games with him as a teammate.

But above all, I reckon, his greatest attribute of all was that he was an outstanding reader of the play. He played mainly a kick behind the play, not ahead of the game. I can always remember seeing him with those long bloody arms coming out of the back pocket, taking the mark. His interception skills were just in a class of their own. They talk these days about that guy from the Eagles, Jeremy McGovern – well Bill was just like that.

When I came into the East Perth side in the mid-'60s, Bill had already been playing for a few years and he was a star. The East Perth/West Perth games were huge; it was a derby-type rivalry that got all the players and all the fans hyped up. There was a lot of sledging on the field, and some of the things that were called over the fence by the fans from both sides – well, let's just say you'd get locked up for it these days.

Bill likes to tell the story of one of those derbies in 1969. I had a good year myself in '69. I won the Sandover, and East Perth played great footy, except for the grand final, where West Perth towelled us up and Bill won his Simpson Medal. But one of the games earlier in the year got a bit fiery. Pol had given him instructions to play on me and play me close, and he must've done something to rile me up.

He reckons I had a swing at him and missed, and he called me a whatever, and it all got a bit heated, to the extent that Bill wanted to carry it on off the field. It may well all be true but I can't remember the details. My memory is that we did carry it on off the field, but in a different way. I thought it was that night but it might have been a week or two down the track. Anyway, we got together and had a few beers. We got to know each other and we've been mates ever since.

That doesn't mean we went any less hard at each other on the field, of course. Playing against him and Polly Farmer was always a challenge. Pol had lost a lot of his speed and leap by that stage. He'd become a real body player. But he'd go off the ball, and on would come Bill. He was all over you like a kangaroo dog, with those long bloody arms, and he could jump a good height off just the one step.

He wasn't above giving you an elbow as you ran in together at a boundary throw-in, but Bill was a scrupulously fair player, a ball player. He didn't have a dirty bone in his body.

When I was growing up, aspiring to be a footballer, my two heroes were John Gerovich and Square Kilmurray. I was lucky enough that my career just overlapped with Square's. My first ever kick in a senior game came off a pass from him. I always liked the fact that he was a hero of Bill's too, something we had in common. And I think Bill and Square had a fair bit in common also. Champion footballers, and just good, straight up and down, no-nonsense blokes.

People do underestimate Bill Dempsey. He was just a great player.

MEL WHINNEN:

They started together at the club as eighteen-year-olds in 1960. They would play seventeen seasons together and go down in club legend as the Cardie Twins. Mel Whinnen won the Breckler Medal as the club's Best and Fairest an astonishing nine times, with Bill finishing second as often as not. In 2018, he was inducted into the Australian Football Hall of Fame. Mel penned this tribute to his 'twin'.

Bill came down to Perth from Darwin as an eighteen-year-old at the instigation of two people: Jack Larcombe, a West Perth recruiter working in Darwin, and Jimmy Anderson, a senior Aboriginal in Darwin and a good footballer himself. Bill had no family or friends in Perth and the move was huge. Jimmy had convinced Bill that he had the responsibility to represent the Darwin Aboriginal football community in Perth and, therefore, he had to be successful – no buts! We can imagine how Jimmy must have felt about that decision at the end of Bill's amazing football career.

As was known at the time, Bill had the necessary footy skills to be successful in Perth but many other men did too. And a lot fell by the wayside. Nobody had it more difficult breaking into a league football team than Bill because of his background and his massive relocation. But whilst many people had their doubts, I don't think Bill saw this situation as a mountain to climb. Rather, he realised, that with help from people at the footy club and friends in Darwin, including his Mum, that there were many benefits to be gained by sticking it out. Bill has always had a happy and a positive temperament and is a 'glass half full' person. This was going to be his difference to others, and to his advantage in adapting to a new life in Perth, and to playing his best footy too.

Bill had a great temperament for footy because he concentrated on the positives in life and didn't look backwards at mistakes. In the tightest of situations, he could smile, crack a joke or get up to a bit of mischief to defuse a confrontation. But such behaviour never affected his strong desperation and determination to win and do well. He was the strongest of competitors. There was the time Mal Brown tossed a glass of water in his face in front of the grandstand at Perth Oval in a close game. Bill flashed his trademark smile, laughed and said, 'I've got you, Brownie.'

Then there was the time Hawthorn's Don Scott, in a state game, got frustrated, and called Bill a 'dago'. Again, there was the smile followed by, 'Scotty, have I got news for you?'

Bill has a great love for his West Perth Football Club and always has. This love reinforced his natural pride and determination and made him an even fiercer competitor. He always gave his utmost because of that love, regardless of the score in the game.

Bill, at six feet three, was often up against much taller players so he had to find ways to compete. He had a natural spring, a flexible torso to weave and twist in a pack and we all reckoned he had telescopic arms that made him nine feet three in ruck and marking contests. Statistics weren't a big deal during our time in footy, but I'd love to know how many marks Bill took in packs in the back pocket, for us over his many years. You could almost hear the mass sigh of relief from our supporters around the ground every time he brought down a screamer to save the day from an opposition attack. He always had a shot at the ruckmen who rested in the forward pocket because they were able to get a rest, he said. When he was spelling in the back pocket he reckoned he was always in the play and didn't have time to rest!

Bill had an excellent dropkick in his early days, and later, the drop punt, on both sides. His high marking was prodigious, with a grip like a vice. His ruckwork was highly effective. And his tackling was as good as you would see anywhere because he was strong and flexible with good reflexes. He didn't like to show off his speed but there were times during his career, particularly early on, when he took off with the goals in sight and surprised everyone with a towering major. These skills, together with his fierce determination, made him the complete player … and a champion. This has been recognised by the players and supporters of every team in the competition.

A remarkable statistic about Bill's football ability is that in seventeen seasons of football and 343 games, he never lost his place in the West Perth Football Club league team through loss of form. This was in Western Australia's elite Aussie Rules competition, the WAFL, in a consistently strong football club, before the inception of the AFL.

Bill was our league team captain for a few years and was one of the best. He set a great example for us to follow and encouraged us at every opportunity. He was so determined but was never reported.

We can imagine how difficult it was for Bill to move to Perth after having spent his formative years in Darwin. But he was a special man. He made friends easily, which helped him settle in. And very importantly, he had great determination to do well at football and in life generally.

We didn't know it at the time but he was always going to succeed. The only problem was this damn cold Perth winter, which was so difficult to get used to. It really was so different to the tropics and had proved the downfall of so many young fellows coming down from the northern areas.

The only way of getting through the winter was to know that he would get back to Darwin at the end of the footy season to get the blood flowing again. And this is what he did year after year.

PART FOUR

THIRTY

I DIDN'T HAVE any post-football blues, or any troubles adjusting to my new life. I just settled into being the full-time manager at Dempsey Day Scaffolding, more hands-on than ever. That was me, really, for the next ten years and a bit. My family and my business.

Our bread and butter was the small- to medium-size jobs: two-storey houses, factories, places like that, sometimes a shopping centre. We were based in Osborne Park, but we'd go anywhere, down to Mandurah, all over Perth. When there was a job on offer, I'd check out the site, look at the plans, and put my quote in. I could beat anyone, most times. We'd sign off, and *bang*, off we'd go.

There were three big companies, Boral and a couple of others, then there was us, and another company also based in Osborne Park run by an Italian feller. So we weren't right at the top of the tree, but we were a serious company in the Perth construction scene. We were pulling in probably about eight hundred grand a year, and we paid for everything, materials, wages, the lot. As we made money, we'd make more frames, and buy more planks, and that determined the profits. We drew a good wage and paid ourselves a bonus from time to time. It was a good business.

As far as I know, I was the only Aboriginal feller in Perth and WA back at that time who was actually an entrepreneur running his own business and employing people. It had started off with just me and Maxie but we got up to twenty-five or more blokes on the payroll. Les's daughter would come in once a week to give a hand with the accounts but otherwise, the running of it was down to me. His two sons Billy and Barry did spells with us too. Barry played footy for West Perth and then Essendon. Other than that, we had all sorts. A lot of blokes came through that company, and they were all just larrikins, happy-go-lucky blokes. To this day, I still see some of them.

We only ever did the one big job in the city, the Ibis Hotel on Murray Street. A scaffolder thinks of a building in terms of frames, not storeys. That one was twenty-five frames high. That's 125 feet. We got it done and I was that happy with myself and all of our guys. We looked at it and said, 'Yeah, we put scaffold all around that.'

That was the scariest job I ever did. We never wore harnesses or anything like that in those days. But I can say that despite scaffolding being a dangerous game, just by its nature, we never had a serious accident at Dempsey Day.

I did have a look at one of the real big jobs, and I thought to myself that we could do this, and I thought I'd try it out. I made an appointment and went and saw one of the managers there at Multiplex. I said, 'Can I look at the plans, and I'll give you a price?'

'What? Now?'

'I can give you a price now; just give me about half an hour.'

So I did a price.

'Not good enough,' he reckoned.

'What d'you mean not good enough? Give me a reason why it isn't.'

I knew it was a good price, even in comparison to the big companies.

He said, 'I shouldn't tell you this, but the BLF told me the price, and that people like you, if you can't meet that price, you don't get the job.'

The BLF – the Builders Labourers Federation – had Multiplex and people like them in their pockets. They didn't want any of the smaller players like us getting those sorts of jobs because they could control the big boys.

So it became pretty clear that we weren't going to break into the really big end of things, but we did alright and we were good at what we did.

OUR LITTLE HOUSEHOLD of three, me and Julie and young Josh, got an addition around this time. Kootji Raymond was a Darwin boy who'd played a bit with the Buffaloes and come down to try out at West Perth. They put him in a flat at Beatty Park, and he enrolled in an arts course at Claremont college. But the footy didn't work out and the club never really looked after him.

I knew his family back in Darwin but I'd never got to know Kootji when he first came down. Maxie, though, he liked to keep an eye on all the Darwin people who came down to Perth, and one day, he said we should look in on Kootji. Well, we found him there in the flat watching TV with two bottles of water in the fridge and nothing else. It was clear he was doing it pretty tough. So we took him out and bought him some tea and gave him a bit of money.

Maxie said to me, 'We've got to do something for this bloke. He can't live like that.'

Long story short: I made a deal with him. As long as he promised that he'd finish the course, I told him he could come and live with us. No rent required, just a bit of a hand around the place, and maybe cook a meal now and then. He's a good cook Kootji. It was a bit like the deal Herb and Ruby Collins had done for me all those years ago in Darwin, only it lasted a bit longer. He was with us for something like four years I reckon. And he did finish his course.

Kootji's a lot younger than me but we just clicked. He's got a good sense of humour and he's a great mimic. He does the best take-off of me making a fool of myself that you can imagine. And he loves all that Territory history, the old stories, and the family stuff. Him and me would yarn for hours. I think that might even be where Josh started to absorb all the stories of my family, listening to me and Kootji yarning at Townshend Street.

I NEVER TURNED my back on footy through this time. I went to every West Perth game, home or away, unless other commitments got in the way. I still loved the club, and the people who were a part of it.

I think the best example of what I mean is Mrs Kelly and Rosa, Rosa Townsend. I never did learn Mrs Kelly's first name; she was just Mrs Kelly. She was a one-eyed Liberal, and Rosa was mad Labor. The two of them sat together at every West Perth game, and they'd argue the toss with each other about any little thing, especially politics, but they both loved the club.

I'd got to know them over the years. I was yarning to

them at a game and they told me I should bring Josh to the footy. So the next home game, I took him along and they told us we had to come and see them after the game. So we did, in the social club there. And they handed an envelope to Josh. He wasn't quite sure what to do, so I told him to open it.

You know what it was? A Commonwealth Bank savings account passbook. They'd opened up an account in Josh's name, and they'd put $343 that they'd saved up from their pensions into it. A dollar for each game I'd played for the club. What a gesture. You just have to love people like that.

The ABC approached me and asked me to join their radio broadcast team as a special comments man. George Grljusich was the head of the team, and Wally Foreman and Dennis Cometti had just started with them. I really enjoyed doing that.

At some point, Johnny Watts approached me and poached me to 6PR. They started up this new football show. Wattsy said he wanted me to come on the panel. He said, 'I've got to tell you from the start, we're not supposed to tell the truth. Make up stories and tell lies,' he said. 'It's about having fun. Talk about football a bit, but not too much.' That suited me right down to the ground.

Gary Carvolth was the MC, and there was Malcolm Brown, Johnny Todd, Wattsy and me. We used to go to all these different pubs and record it on a Friday, then play it back on Saturday. I got paid for it, plus they dressed us, and the free food and grog. We used to have some fun on that show.

Then in 1985, my old mate Windows, John Wynne, came back to West Perth as the senior coach. We'd played together before he went over to South Australia. He asked if I could give him a hand.

'What d'you mean give you a hand?'

'Can you come and coach the reserves and be the chairman of selectors?'

'Oh no, really, I don't want to do that. I just want to go to the footy and watch it.'

But I caved in, of course, and did my only coaching stint, with the West Perth reserves, for the '85 and '86 seasons.

The reserves got nothing. It was all about the league players. So I roped in my two mates. I made Stan Hart the official general manager of the reserves, and I made Ron Biok the boss of the social side of it. And Peter Curley, another old Cardie player – his son Todd went on to play for them too – I made him the runner. So I was surrounded by all these mates. We were all doing it for the love; no one was getting paid.

We went round to all the local businesses asking for donations, so we could encourage the boys and give them something after the game. The pizza bloke used to give us all these pizzas after the game, stuff like that.

I enjoyed it on the whole, and we went alright, without winning flags or anything. It was a happy team. But I just wasn't cut out for coaching. I got too emotional. I couldn't get used to them losing. I couldn't handle that. So I told Wynney that I'd done my bit and to get someone else to coach the reserves.

I had a few other things on my mind too. 1986 wasn't a good year for me.

THIRTY-ONE

IT ALL STARTED the day one of the BLF organisers came to see me at the yard in Osborne Park. I don't have the records any more but I reckon this must've been in 1986. I've always had it in my mind that Dempsey Day went for sixteen years, which would make it 1971 to 1986. And I can remember that Josh had started coming in to do odd jobs around the yard for us on the weekends for some pocket money. Him and Billy Day's son would come in. He'd just started high school, which would make him around thirteen.

All of our blokes were in the union and paid their dues, and I got on pretty well with most of the organisers. But this bloke said to me, 'Look, we've got these three New Zealand blokes. They're scaffolders, and you've got to put them on.'

I said, 'We don't need any scaffolders. We've got a heap of our own.'

'Well, you'll just have to fit them in. Just give it a go.'

'We don't need them. We've got our own guys.'

'Just as a favour,' he said.

So I said I'd give them a try-out for a week, and if they were okay, we'd think about it. I sent them out to a job we had going on a shopping centre at North Beach.

By morning tea time on the first day, the bloke who was running the site rang me up. I knew this feller. He said, 'Bill, what have you done to me?'

'What do you mean?'

'The BLF have just been here, and they've shut the site down.'

'What for?'

'Those three guys that you sent here, they started picking holes with the scaffolding. The organiser's come and said it's all got to be redone. You know the consequences.'

'Yeah, I do.'

In those days, the easiest way to get at the contractors and the builders was through the scaffold. Once the scaffold stopped, the job stopped, but the builder was still supposed to pay every labourer on site until it's sorted out, and there must've been about a hundred blokes on that site. That's how the BLF used to operate. They had some sort of problem with this builder. So they go and get me to put on some of their guys, and the very first morning they're on the job, they get the site shut down. I don't know for sure, but my guess is that they probably removed some of the handrails themselves, then called in their organiser mate.

So the site manager was desperate when he rang me up. He wanted to know when he'd be able to start again. I said, 'Tell those three bastards to come back to the office and I'll sort them out.'

When they showed up, I said, 'Thanks very much. I gave you a chance and you shit in my face.'

'No, the scaffolding wasn't right,' they reckoned.

'You guys were there. Why didn't you fix it?'

They had no answer.

'I've made up your pay. Grab it and piss off. Don't come back here again.'

'You can't do that.'

'I just did. You want to carry on with it, let me know. Only too happy to oblige.'

The next day the organiser came back with four big Maori blokes. I was expecting them. I knew they'd come. Everyone was out; I was in the office by myself. 'What's your trouble?' I asked.

'Those three blokes, you sacked them yesterday.'

'Yes. I sacked them. They helped shut down the site. They didn't do their job of rectifying that scaffold, so tell me why I shouldn't have sacked them. Until I can organise something, they're just going to cost us money, not you. We're in the shit with the contractor, thanks to you. Who's going to pay for all this? Obviously you're not going to put your hand up, because you caused the trouble.'

He was only a short little bloke, but these big Maori blokes came up and were standing around me. I picked up this piece of scaffold pipe I had in the office. I stood up, and I said, 'If you're going to cause any trouble, I'll be ready.' And I went *bang* with the pipe on the desk.

They all looked at me.

The organiser said, 'You've got to put them back on.'

'No, I'm not putting them back on. If they ever come back round here again, I'll kick them out. I gave them a chance, and they go and do that. You've obviously got something going against that company, so you use the scaffold to get to them. Our scaffold. We've got nothing to do with your argument with him. We're the innocent bystanders.'

And that's how it started.

Next thing I know, there's a picket line out the front on

the grounds we've sacked scaffolders with no good cause. People were going past the picketers throwing eggs at them and calling them mongrels, so they gave up on that. But the damage was done.

The BLF did nothing to us directly after that, but they got a list of all our clients and went round to all of them and said to them, 'If you want trouble, keep using Dempsey Day Scaffolding, because we're going to destroy them.'

And that's what happened.

They went to Cyclone, the company that used to supply a lot of the fittings, and said, 'Don't supply Dempsey Day Scaffolding with any gear.' They even controlled the people who were selling the wood, the fourteen-foot scaffold planks.

They were just deadly. They had the whole situation stitched up. People used to be shit-scared of them.

Maxie dropped off some scaffold on a Friday at Swanbourne. The BLF were running the show there and they said, 'No, you can't drop it off; you've got to come back Monday, because we've shut the site down.'

He said he was dropping it off whether they liked it or not. 'It's my last job before I knock off. I don't need a hand. I can do it myself.'

There wasn't a lot of scaffold, so they just let him go, and he unloaded. Next Saturday afternoon, he's sitting in the Barleycorn with all his mates, having a drink and a bet, and three big burly BLF blokes walked in and king-hit him from behind. Because he defied them.

They didn't even front him. They hit him from behind. And he was only a skinny little bloke. They put him in hospital.

One by one, our clients gave way. I knew a lot of those builders. Some of them were good West Perth guys. And they said, 'Sorry Bill, we can't. We don't need the trouble. We're just hanging on by the skin of our teeth anyway.'

We had to start letting all the blokes go, we were just bleeding money. Most of them had families and mortgages. And they had to go and try to find something else to replace what they had, thanks to the BLF.

And they didn't let up. Some of their hoods came round, and went down the back of the yard. We were down to two fellers left on the payroll. Maxie, who'd started it all off with me sixteen years earlier, and Derek Kickett, who'd just started playing with West Perth. They see these two Indigenous guys working there, and told them they had to stop work and get out of there.

Maxie said to them, 'You can get knotted. That's my brother up there in the office. This is Derek Kickett. And we're staying here to support him, so why don't you bugger off!'

But it was all over. Les and I sat down and looked at our options, and there weren't any. We couldn't beat them, because they were too strong. We just decided that that was it. Just like that, the company folded. It was hardly four weeks since the blue had started.

I'VE BEEN ASKED since whether we tried to get any help or backing from the government. It was Brian Burke who was in power at the time.

I grew up as a Labor man, from when I was a kid at the mission. The Labor party in those days were really good to us mission kids. A lot of my relations were Labor people. And the Buffaloes, most of them were Labor. Maxie was, and my mates Ron and Stan. Even though I was an owner of the company, I paid my union dues and I worked hands-on at our sites. But we would've been bashing our heads against a brick wall.

The BLF were all about control. They had all the big construction companies in their pockets, and it was all very cosy. They didn't like the smaller guys like us at the best of times. Then they used me to get at another company they had in their sights. And because we wouldn't play ball with the BLF, they destroyed us. They could, and they did. It was as simple as that.

The land and buildings belonged to Les. The assets were basically only the trucks and frames. After sixteen years, I left Les to do the wind-up, and walked away with virtually nothing. All that hard work down the drain.

THIRTY-TWO

IN THE AFTERMATH of the collapse of Dempsey Day, I did something I'd been thinking about for quite a while. For all of his life, I'd been talking to Josh about all of my family, his family, up there in the Territory. Not just our blood family, but all my other family too, the Retta Dixon gang, my brother boys and sister girls. He'd met quite a few them, people coming and going between Darwin and Perth. But he'd never been there; he'd never met them all; he'd never seen any of them on their home ground and smelled that Territory air. Julie had her reservations but she agreed to let me take him home.

We set off on a journey. Not just me and Josh. I took along my other two brother boys, Stan the mad Irishman and Ron the crazy Croat. They'd been hearing my Territory stories all the years we'd known each other and were always telling me they wanted to go up there and see it for themselves, so I told them to come along. Me and Josh and Stan and Ron flew to Darwin.

Mum was living down in Katherine at that time, so I didn't want to get tangled up in Darwin. I knew if I went to see anyone there, it'd just snowball and we'd never get away. Kootji was back in Darwin at the time, so I lined him up to have a car loaded up with tucker and ready to go from the airport. We landed, we picked up the car, and we headed south down the Stuart highway. We got into Katherine just as the sun was going down.

Like I think I said earlier, Mum just worshipped the ground that Josh walked on, and it was so good to connect those two up properly. But there were so many things that happened on that trip that stirred the emotions for all of us.

Mum had met Ron and Stan before when she came to Perth and she knew how close I was to them. She also knew, from me, that both of them had lost their mothers. She pointed at me, then looked them in the eye and said, 'What do you call him?'

That's our brother, was their answer.

'Well, if he's your brother, I'm your mother. You've got to call me mother.'

They looked at me. I told them yes, that's what people here do; she just claimed you. And they've called her mother ever since. It gave me a bit of a jolt when Mum did that. I wasn't expecting it.

The place Mum was in then in Katherine was one of those big old Territory houses with most of the rooms upstairs – like the place of Herb and Ruby Collins in Darwin that I'd stayed in when I left the mission. She set about settling us all in. She showed Josh and Stan and Ron where their beds were. I asked her, 'Where am I sleeping?'

'Downstairs with the dogs,' she said.

Nothing changes, hey. There was a squeeze on for space and beds, and she made me one up in the downstairs room. It wasn't a problem at all, but she still liked to stir me up.

There was a big party that night. All the Katherine family

were there, the Holtze descendants, and half of the rest of Katherine too, I reckon. Everybody was charged up, and as happens at such times, this huge fight broke out. Josh and the boys were a bit wide-eyed; they'd never seen anything like it before. I got them into a quiet corner and told them not to worry, it'd all be over shortly. Which of course, it was. Fifteen minutes later it was all over, and everybody was all over us, apologising and embracing.

The party finally wound down, and everybody's in bed, me downstairs on my own, when I hear a noise, and someone singing out for me. It was Ando, Jimmy the King. 'We heard all about you, hightailing it out of Darwin. We're all here to see you. Everyone's coming down. Don't you worry about tucker, or meat, or anything. It's all organised.'

I couldn't believe it. A big mob of the Retta Dixon crew came down to Katherine. They got hold of a killer, and brought down all the other necessities and we had this big get-together down at the old low-level crossing there at Katherine. Josh sat there with me, and they all came up in ones and twos and I introduced them to him, and told him their names. There were big embraces, big hugs. And Josh knew them all, from the stories I'd told him over the years. I'd tell him a name, and he'd call their nickname: that's Wewak, that's Watermelon, and so on and so forth. They were all pretty impressed, and pretty pleased. I was so proud of him.

And then there was Nancy, my Mum's sister-in-law. She was the one who'd taken me and held me as a newborn when Mum rejected me at first. Me and Josh and Mum were walking down the main street in Katherine. The shops there had these big wide verandahs, and the Aboriginal people would sit there in the shade, right there on the main street. Mum said to Josh, 'Hang on, hang on.' There was this old lady sitting on a blanket, and Mum stopped and started talking to her in language. She got Josh by the hand and pulled him over, and said to Nancy, 'Who's this young boy?'

'This one's from Billy,' the old girl said.

Mum said to Josh, 'Help her up, help her up.'

I was feeling a bit nervous. I thought he might feel embarrassed. He'd never seen or mixed with a big heap of blackfellers before. But he grabbed hold of her, and she started howling and crying, and grabbed hold of him, kissing him and everything.

He looked over her shoulder and said to me, 'This is Nancy?'

'That's her.'

I'd told him the story, and he'd remembered it.

Josh was a bit freaked out by it all but he took everything in his stride. And he was real proud. To be who he was. To meet all our people. Especially his grandmother, and all his uncles and aunties, and that old lady Nancy.

I'd been a bit worried but he took it all in his stride. I was just over the moon and so proud of him.

Josh wanted to see Birdum. He'd heard all my stories about the place, and he wanted to see where I'd been born. It started off as just me and my mates and Josh and Mum. But somehow it snowballed, and there was twelve cars that set off from Katherine to Birdum. More members of the Holtze clan than you could poke a stick at.

I hadn't been back there since I was a kid. There's not much left of Birdum now, just the big old water tank from the railway line. At Granny and Grandpa's old camp, all the buildings were gone. There was just the odd rusty bed frame and that sort of thing that you find at old bush camps.

Everybody was looking round trying to find the tree, the

tree where I'd been born. Mum sung out to Josh. 'This is it,' she told him. 'The tree's gone, but this stump here, this is the tree where your father was born.'

Josh was that pleased. It clearly meant a lot to him. He got a texta out, and he wrote on that stump. 'Bill Dempsey, 17 March 1942.'

There was another big moment on that trip too, something that meant a lot to me. It was one of the reasons I'd had to take him to the Territory. I took Josh and the fellers out to my grandmother Moondoolooloo's country, the Roper River.

There's a crossing on the river that goes over to the community where my grandmother grew up. We pulled up there, and there were three blokes there fishing for barramundi. They were reeling them in, putting them in this great big icebox. They were fishing from the shore, not standing in the river, because the Roper is full of crocodiles as well as barras.

I explained things to Josh. I told him that the Roper is a sacred river for his great-grandmother's people, the Ngalakan people. Like the Ganges in India for the people there. This is her sacred river. I told him he had to jump into that river.

'But Dad, there's crocodiles in there.'

And Stan and Ron were backing him up, saying I couldn't make him do that. But I explained that I'd done it when I was a kid. That it was important.

'You don't have to stay in there. Just jump in and jump out, but you've got to go right under the water.'

And he did.

'Now you're right,' I told him. 'Your great-grandmother would be very proud of you.'

It was a good experience.

After the dramas I'd been through back in Perth, that whole trip was a good experience. For me. For my two Perth brothers, Ron and Stan. And for Josh.

Julie had been a bit reluctant about it, and I hadn't been at all sure how he'd handle it. But we misjudged him. He had it in him.

THE TERRITORY HAD got into Josh's blood, which I was quietly pleased about. A few years later, when he'd finished year twelve, he didn't want to go straight into an everyday job or anything like that. He packed everything he had into a car, and drove himself to Darwin, and lived up there for a year or so, working here and there, and reconnecting with everyone. The Retta Dixon mob just loved him.

I remember one time he rang me up. He told me he was staying with his Nana. 'She told me I've got to stay here so she can keep an eye on me.'

'And what about the King? Did you go and see the King?' I asked him.

'Yeah, I did.'

'And what happened?'

'Jimmy said, "Good to see you son," and asked me what my plans were while I was in Darwin. I told him that I want to find some work and play a bit of footy. I told him I had a couple of mates I'd met who were playing for Nightcliff.'

He liked to be a smart-arse sometimes, young Josh. Hence the crack about Nightcliff. Jimmy just looked at him and said, 'It's very hard to play with two broken legs.'

I told him I wouldn't have been game to say that to Jimmy.

I made it up there for his first game with the Buffaloes. I was standing there with Jimmy Anderson and Wewak when he played his first game in the reserves and ran out there in the double blue colours. Jimmy, he looked away from me. He was real emotional, like I was. Jimmy had a tear in his eye, and he's a real tough man.

THIRTY-THREE

YOU MAY HAVE noticed the dedication that I made at the start of this book. It is to my five children, Marinda, Raelene, Nalita, Karen and Josh. So far, I've only mentioned one of them, my son Josh. I've got some explaining to do and it's a little bit complicated. I was going to leave this part to the end. I thought it might be a way to wrap things up with what, to me, is a happy ending. But even if it is pretty hard to explain, these things are too important, too big a part of my life to just tack on at the end. So before I get to life after Dempsey Day Scaffolding, there's a story to tell.

You wouldn't want to know how many hours, how many evenings, how many glasses of red, I've spent pondering over the things I'm about to describe. I've tried to work out whether it means anything, whether it throws any light on what sort of feller I am or not. But I haven't come up with any answers. All I can do is shake my head and say it is strange but true.

As I said, so far I've only mentioned Josh. The other four, my daughters, didn't come along in a rush late in my life. In fact, Josh, the only one who I grew up, is the youngest of my five children. The other four are big sisters to him. It is one of the blessings of my life that he thinks of them in that way. It's just that he didn't find out about them, and neither did I, until much further down the track. And each one of the four has her own story.

It is hard to do justice to their stories here, because each of them has a life that in a sense has nothing to do with me. But I can't tell my story without including them in it; they have become a part of me. And one of the reasons I wanted to put my own story down is to give them and their loved ones and their kids the backstory of this part of their own lives.

IT IS HARD to know where to start with all of this. There is the historical order of events, but that only comes with the benefit of hindsight. I think the way to go is with the way it all unfolded for me. The exact order of things and the dates around them are hard to pin down but I'll give it my best shot.

It should be clear by now that I didn't lead the life of a monk until I settled down with Julie. I had plenty of girlfriends through the 1960s. But I certainly never thought of myself as a womaniser. I watched all my brother boys settling into marriages and relationships and having kids and that's what I wanted for myself. I imagined myself settling back in Darwin with a family, my boys hopefully playing for the Buffaloes, and the girls doing whatever they wanted in life. But it just never seemed to work out for me until Julie came along. It was four years into our marriage before we had Josh, but when he arrived in the world, I couldn't have been happier.

Then, through the '80s, my escapades of the '60s started coming back to bite me on the bum. I don't know of anyone else who's experienced anything quite like this.

The first one to make contact with me was Raelene. I'd been seeing her mum on and off during one of my annual trips back to the Territory. This would have been the mid-'60s. The following year, when I was back in Darwin again, I discovered that she'd gotten married and that she had a little girl. I knew the feller that she married. That was fine; we were both getting on with our lives, and to tell you the truth, I didn't think a lot more about it.

But when Raelene was sixteen, her mother told her that the man she was married to was not her father – I was. Naturally, Raelene was pretty pissed off and she kicked up a hell of a stink. Her mother had never told me. I was completely in the dark until I got a call from this sixteen-year-old girl. I met up with her, of course, once I knew. All I can really say is that it wasn't easy at first, for any of us.

NALITA WAS NEXT. She came into my life not that long after Raelene did. The beginning of the story is sort of similar but it panned out very differently. I met Nalita's mum in Darwin, I think it must have been the year after my affair with Raelene's mum. She came from Alice Springs, she already had two kids, and she was gorgeous.

As I would eventually find out, Nalita was born from that affair, and she was adopted out, and grew up in Adelaide. When Nalita turned seventeen, she started wanting to know who her real father was and asking her adoptive parents. She traced her mother, and found her way to Alice Springs, where her aunties told her that if she really wanted to know who her father was, she should go to Darwin; she might find out up there.

So she goes to Darwin. She's in a pub, and this young

bloke sees her. They got talking, and he said to her, 'My dad's having a party tonight, a barbeque, do you want to come along with me?'

'Will your folks mind?'

'No, no, you'll be right.'

Well that boy was Mango Anderson, son of Jimmy Anderson. The two of them get to Jimmy's place, and Mango says, 'Dad, I hope you don't mind, I met this girl at the pub, and I've invited her to the party.'

Before Nalita could say a word, Jimmy Anderson said, 'I know you.'

'No, you don't know me. This is my first time in Darwin. I grew up in Adelaide and I've just come here.'

'No, no. When I say I know you, I know who you are.'

'Well, who am I?'

'You're the daughter of Bill Dempsey.'

He'd known Nalita's mother back when the two of us were going out. And he just knew straight away from the look of her.

She said, 'That's why I'm here in Darwin. That's who I'm looking for.'

Ando rang me up. 'Get up here you bastard. I've just found your daughter.'

So I headed straight up to Darwin and I met Nalita.

That was two women I'd hooked up with in Darwin who kept their daughters away from me. I never knew about either of them.

I'M BACK IN Perth, in blissful ignorance of the seeds that I'd sown, getting on with my footy career, and working at Humes, when I meet this gorgeous Indigenous girl, and naturally, one thing led to another. It was all going along nicely until I made a big blue. I completely stuffed up; it's something which I regret to this day. We parted.

Let me make it clear, this was before I'd met Julie. I have to say, in my own defence, these things were happening one after the other, not all at the same time.

Anyway, the years go by. I get invited to the Aboriginal ball, the big do they have every year as part of NAIDOC week. I'm sitting there at a table with all these people from one of the big families. I knew them all, more or less, except for this pretty girl sitting next to me. I leaned over, and whispered to the feller who'd invited me, 'Who's this girl that I'm sitting next to?'

'That's your daughter. Marinda.'

Holy shit!

I discovered that a lot of the local mob knew the story. But not me. Just like with Raelene and Nalita, I didn't have the faintest clue until that day at the NAIDOC ball.

So that made three. Three Aboriginal women who'd carried children by me but had chosen not to tell me. Three daughters I hadn't known about.

These three discoveries, if you can call them that, came *boom, boom, boom*, all in the space of two or three years. I was a single man again by that time. Julie and I had separated.

I wondered, 'What the hell?' I was trying to work out if there was something wrong with me. I couldn't believe it was happening to me.

I GOT A bit of a breather after that, but it wasn't over.

Early on in my time in Perth, I'd met this nurse. We went out for about three months and then she vanished. I never saw her again. I knew a couple of her friends, and I asked them what had happened. They told me she'd gone back to New South Wales where she came from. You know the story by now; I had no choice but to just get on with my life.

A few years after these other three shocks to my system, I get a mystery phone call one day. It's a young woman, in her mid-thirties.

'My name is Karen. I was adopted out from the hospital when I was born in Sydney. There's something I'd like to ask you.'

Karen's story was that she'd grown up with a really nice family. She knew who her mother was because it was on her birth certificate, which she'd been able to get hold of. But that certificate said 'father unknown'.

Eventually her mother told her my name but she didn't want to go into it any more than that. Karen had a sister in her adoptive family, and they talked about it a lot, going backwards and forwards, thinking about how they might find this bloke with nothing but a name.

Well, Karen was a mad computer person, and when Google started to become a thing, one day she bit the bullet and googled the name. She came across a picture of me in the 1975 grand final, with big curly hair, holding the trophy up.

She just said to her sister, 'Google him and tell me. Google Bill Dempsey.'

Once her sister had done that, she told her, 'Go and get him. That's him.'

So Karen rang me.

That's how it went with the fourth one.

When I rang Joshua up and said I had something to tell him, he said, 'Don't tell me I've got another sister!' And he did!

Karen was born in 1964. She is the oldest of my children, and she was the last to find me.

What can I say? I'm not proud of how things happened, but I am happy that they have all met up.

IT'S NOT REALLY my business to tell you all about the four girls and their mothers, and how everything panned out for them all. Of course it's not all a story of wine and chocolates. But I will say this. I got to know all four of them, and Josh has met them all too, and we both think of them all as family. I am so glad that each of them found me. They have made my life richer.

It's not that long ago that I went and spent three weeks with Karen and her family at Dungog in NSW where she lives. It was the second time I'd been over to stay with her. We'd be walking down the street and people would look at us and smile, and say, 'That's your Dad alright.'

I could say I've got no regrets, but I do regret with those girls that I never grew any of them up. The only one I was able to grow up was Josh, and he's the baby. And all the girls love him.

Apart from Marinda, the other three all got to meet Mum. Raelene and Nalita were there in Darwin, so it was easy for them to make it happen. With Karen, it was a bit harder, and a bit different. The other two girls had been teenagers when it happened, but Karen was a grown woman, and she didn't have any connection to the Territory at all. But she wanted to go up there. She wanted to meet her grandmother. She asked if I would be there, and I said yes, of course. So Karen and her husband made the big trip up to the Territory, and I went up too.

I was expecting to cop it from Mum. As all these stories had come out, with the other three girls, she'd let rip at me, calling me a mongrel this, and a so and so that. That was just her way and I didn't take offence at all. I think what really upset her was that she had missed out on seeing these granddaughters of hers growing up, the way she'd been able to see all her other grandies, all my nieces and nephews.

But by the time Karen and her husband came up, Mum was getting on and getting a bit frail. She was on a walking stick, and unsteady on her feet, and I could see she was nervous, which wasn't really like Mum. I introduced them, and we all sat down, and had a really good yarn. It was good.

After a while, Karen said that they had booked a tour to see a bit of Darwin. She said they would be back to see her again, but they had to take off for now. 'Yes, yes, go and have a look at Darwin,' she told them, and saw them out the door. I thought that was going to be the signal for a blue to end all blues. But Mum just started crying. She was a very strong woman, but she just started crying. Karen looks a bit like Mum.

LATER ON, ON that same visit, I took Karen to meet all the Retta Dixon crew. I said, 'Look, I've got to introduce you to all these girls over here; they're all girls I grew up with on the mission. Come on. I'll take you over there now.'

As we were walking over to them, one of the ladies stood up and said, 'Karen, we know who you are just from looking at you, you don't have to tell us.' She looked at me and said, 'Bill, piss off. Karen, come and sit here and we're going to tell you all about him.' I shook my head and left them to it.

Karen freaked out. She couldn't believe how many

relations she had in the world. And that to me was the icing on the cake. I thought to myself, I've made a mess of things as far as relationships go, but at least some good has come out of it all, with those four beautiful women, and of course, my son Josh.

I've never managed to get all five of my kids under the one roof at the one time. But four of them, all except Marinda, made it to Darwin for my mother's funeral.

I DID SAY that this part of my story is a bit complicated. That's an understatement, you might say; it's almost as complicated as it gets, and I guess it sounds mighty strange when all the beans get spilled in one rush like this.

As I also said, I've spent more hours than you can count pondering it all. But I never found any answers. And, you know, in the end, I didn't care what other people thought of me, because I never planned it to be like that.

I just wanted to be an ordinary guy, have a wife and family and enjoy life. It never worked out that way. The only one I married was Joshua's mother, Julie, and me and her finished up separating.

I've made my peace with all of my children. I love them all, and my life is better for knowing them all. I have regrets, for sure, but I have to live with them.

THIRTY-FOUR

AFTER THAT TRIP to the Territory, I had to work out what I was going to do with myself. I had a footy career and sixteen years of running a good little business behind me. But I was still only in my mid-forties; I had responsibilities and I had virtually nothing to my name.

I came up with an answer, even if it did mean a pretty big change in my life. That answer was Warark. Warark is the crow. That is my name, my dreaming. I set up a building company called Warark. After all those years with Dempsey Day, I knew my way around the building game and the idea was to set up a company building houses for Aboriginal communities.

I couldn't do it in my own right, because I didn't have a builder's licence. But I got introduced to a feller who had the licence, and already had a group of companies, and we set it up under his umbrella, with his company guaranteeing the finances when we put in for tenders.

That's how it worked. The government would allocate money to build a house, or a number of houses in a community, and there'd be a tender process to get the gig to build them. My partner handled the government side and the tendering, and I ran everything else. So we kicked it off, and slowly, slowly, one house at a time – just the same way I'd got Dempsey Day off the ground – we started to build it up.

It was a Kimberley business. We did a few places around Derby and Broome, but mostly it was in and around Fitzroy Crossing, the Fitzroy Valley as they call it. We built houses at Noonkanbah, Junjuwa, Darlngunaya, down near the Old Crossing there, and a heap of other places.

I set myself up in a van at the caravan park next door to the supermarket there. We had an arrangement with a feller who had a block in the light industrial area; he gave us some space there and we used a part of his yard as a depot and an operations centre. And we had a gang of tradies and labourers. Most of the labourers were local, and the tradies came in from Broome or Derby; a lot of them were Indigenous fellers. At its peak, I reckon we had about twenty fellers working with us. We were training up apprentices. It was like a big family sort of a thing.

I was the one who found all the work, and then we tendered for it. And if we got the tender, I ran everything from that point on: managing the site, taking care of all the ordering and the organising of the tradies and their subcontracts, keeping the wages book and the accounts book, the whole lot.

I really enjoyed that era of my life. I was perfectly happy there on my own in the caravan park. You made good friends, met beautiful people. Fitzroy was a pretty rough and ready old town. It reminded me of my hometown Darwin, and the old days at the Parap Hotel. You want to fight – go down to the Crossing Inn. And if you don't want to fight, you can see the fights. I never used to go to the Fitzroy River Lodge. I used to always go to the Crossing Inn, because that's where the local people were, and I enjoyed their company. And jeez, they used to cook some good food there. I used to love the food they had.

I made a couple of good mates in Derby, Johnny Brahim and Jimmy Greatorex. They joined my list of brother boys. Most weekends, unless there was something important to do on the work front, I'd take off into Derby and get into mischief with them.

Just like Dempsey Day, it was a good little business. And I believed in what we were doing, building houses for the mob, employing lots of locals and hanging out with the Fitzroy people. But it's the story of my life. Nothing lasts forever.

My partner went bust. It was nothing to do with Warark – we were going along nicely – it was the other companies in his group. I could say more, but let's just leave it at saying I wasn't very bloody happy at the time. So I'm left trying to run a company that's still got contracts to build houses, a bunch of fellers working and contracting for us, but no cash flow. Most of the contracts were with the Department of Housing. Their terms had started off at thirty-one days after invoice for payment. But then it had stretched out to forty-five days. Meantime, I've got all these guys on the payroll. Half of them were married, or had a family, married or not. They had commitments, they had mortgages, they were paying off vehicles or whatever. They needed money every week. So it used to be a battle.

I was forever ringing the Department of Housing to see if they would pay us a bit of money so we could keep going, but they didn't give a damn, and my so-called partner was playing silly buggers. And I'm left singing in the rain.

You don't know how hard I tried to keep that business alive. I went down to Perth and made an appointment with the feller in charge of the Department of Housing. But he wanted to talk footy and all he could say was the rules were the rules as far as payments went. I went to the banks. I went to ATSIC. But all they could talk about was security and I had none.

I waved the contracts at them. I told them I wasn't after grants or anything like that. I just needed to cover my cash flow. We had contracts worth nearly two million to do. Two jobs. I said, 'Look, here's the government contract worth two million. All I want is a cash flow of $150,000, and we will pay you back, with interest.'

'What's your assets?'

'Don't these documents, government documents, stand for us?'

'No.'

Not even ATSIC that was supposed to support Aboriginal people to go into business would support me.

Then the last straw was my meeting with the big boss at the Department of Housing. I could read between the lines that he wasn't going to do anything. So I said, 'Look, I was brought up to be an honest man. I was brought up to respect people. I'm going to have to go now, because if I don't, I'm going to knock your head clean off your shoulders.' And I walked out the door.

I had no wife and no house in Perth by this time, after years in the Kimberley. When I walked out that door, I only had the clothes I stood up in and my car. That's all I had.

THIRTY-FIVE

A WEEK LATER, the feller in charge of the Department of Housing's secretary rang me up and said he wanted me to come in for a meeting.

'Does he want me to come back and knock his head off?'

But she kept on at me, said it was really important. I knew her a little bit, and knew she was good-hearted, and she talked me into it, reluctantly. The next week, I went in and sat down in his office.

'Bill, I understand your problem.'

'Do you?'

'I can't help you by bringing forward payments, that's the government way of doing business.'

'Well, what do you want me in here for?'

'We're starting up a section here. It's going to be called the Aboriginal Housing Directorate.'

'So?'

'I want you to be part of this directorate. We want to have at least 75 per cent Aboriginal people in it. With your expertise and your reputation, we think you'll be good for this department.'

And that's how I became a public servant for the first time in my life, at the age of fifty-something.

I SUPPOSE YOU could say that I'm a feller who thinks government gets things wrong more often than they get it right, especially when it comes to working with Aboriginal people. But the Aboriginal Housing Directorate was a damned good program, even if I say so myself.

There were five of us when we started. We had to work everything out as we went along. We had to make up the program, and we did it as a team. We learned by going out and talking to people. Essentially, we were project managers. The five of us each got a different region, and I got the best one, the Kimberley.

Our brief wasn't new buildings, but repair and maintenance of the existing housing stock out in Aboriginal communities. And the philosophy was to empower the people in the communities to do that work themselves, and to make the decisions for themselves about what needed to be done and how it would be done. And it worked. Really well.

I RENTED A place in Perth, on Jersey Street. Kootji Raymond and I hooked up again. He moved in with me there in Jersey Street, which was really good. He'd got into filmmaking by this time, and we finished up doing a documentary together about the history of our old club. *Buffalo Legends*, it was called.

There was someone else who came into my life in a big way too. I'd first met Jeran, Jeran McPartland, whilst I was still living up in the Kimberley, trying to make a go of Warark.

She was a real rock for me during all the hard times of that falling to pieces.

And once I moved back down to Perth, we saw more of each other. At some point there, I moved out of Jersey Street, into Jeran's place. I'm still there today. She's been the most wonderful partner for over twenty years now, in this last phase of my life. I've been with Jeran now for longer than any other person in my life.

But back then, mostly I was on the road, basing myself again in Fitzroy Crossing, and starting up and managing the projects we got going. At its peak, I think there was something like fourteen different communities I was working with. Mowanjum, Kurnangki, Junjuwa, Bayulu, Djugerari, Noonkanbah, Kadjina at Milijidee, Wangkatjunka, and a bunch of others.

I'd do up an itinerary, base myself at Fitzroy, and I'd cover something like 3,000 kilometres on a round trip, with probably half of that off-road. We called it the Management Support Program. By jeez I loved that work. What made it really loveable was that you helped people to help themselves. I think the best way I can explain it is to tell the story of Kurnangki, a community right there in Fitzroy Crossing, opposite the roadhouse.

KURNANGKI WEREN'T THE first mob I worked with. In fact, I had a few meetings there and they seemed sort of reluctant about taking part. Then I got yarning with the chairman's son down at the pub and asked him what the problem was.

'A lot of them come from the desert, and they're not really educated, you know, can't read and write. They're feeling a bit shamed. They wouldn't know how to read a plan, or measure things, and all that.'

Well, I got him to organise another meeting for the next morning before I had to go back to Derby. And I explained the philosophy of the program to them.

'Everything is in your hands. You mob make the decisions, not me. When we start off, we have to get a supervisor-type bloke, and he's got to be qualified. He'll be on our payroll, but when we place an advertisement, we'll bring three blokes here, but then you make the decision on which one you want. I've got no input. You pick that man. You pick your gang of six to eight men to work with him. You pick which house you're going to work on – my advice is to start on the worst one first. You make the decisions, right down to picking the paint for that house, not the supervisor – you pick it. You tell the supervisor what you want from him, and if you don't like him, you can sack him.'

They were still mumbling away. So I said, 'There's a couple of other things I should tell you. When you start your first house, if it takes three months from start to finish, so be it. And the other thing is, that for any of you who don't understand about looking at plans and measuring and all that, we're going to teach you.'

'True?'

'Yes, that's part of the deal.'

Well *bang*, off they went. They picked their team and they started off. The bloke they picked as the supervisor was a German feller who lived in Broome. He hadn't done a lot of work with Aboriginal people, but I talked him through how it was all supposed to work, and he was the right man for the job.

The house they decided to start with – there was a girl in a wheelchair living in it, and she was finding it hard to get in and out of the house. I said they could put a ramp in if they wanted and knock down walls if they got council permission. 'You decide; we'll cater for it.'

They walked me through that house when it was ready to hand over. It was transformed. Walls were knocked out, doors were changed. They'd made a ramp, not a steep one, so that girl could just go straight in. She was a very happy girl. And the thing that really impressed me, the house was like a painting. No room was the same, no wall was the same. So colourful, it was like a painting.

I gathered all those boys together and we had lunch. 'It's the first one, and I'm very impressed,' I told them. 'But I've got a funny feeling that every time I go away, you mob get some gardiya (whitefella) contractors to come in here and do the work.'

The supervisor was looking at me, appalled, because he'd been telling me I had to give the team a big pat on the back. 'Tell him; tell him,' all the boys were saying to him.

I gave them a smile that let them know I was just stirring them up and said, 'But guess what? There's eighteen more to go.'

They just took off that gang. They transformed the village. They got themselves shirts and caps made up with 'Kurnangki MSP Team' on them and were walking around with their chests stuck out. They wanted people to be able to cook outside, and the supervisor got a metalworker mate in Broome to design a barbecue out of a forty-four-gallon drum that you put a whole kangaroo inside to cook. Everybody wanted one of them.

THIRTY-SIX

ONE OF THE nice things about being a public servant after all those years of running my own companies was getting regular holidays, with the pay cheque still coming in, and not having to worry about the company and the workers while I was away.

I got the chance to tie up a few of the loose threads of my life.

One of them was Wewak's wedding. It was supposed to happen back in 1964. He'd come down to try out with West Perth that year. He was a pretty decent footballer, Wewak, and I reckoned he was a fair chance to make it. But he'd only been down about a month when he came to see me. 'Brother, I'm in big trouble,' he said.

'Oh yeah, what?'

'I got a letter from Shirley and she's pregnant. What should I do?'

'Look, if I tell you what to do, you're going to come back in later years and tell me, "You told me to do that." So I'm telling you nothing.'

'Okay, let me put it another way. What would you do if it was you?'

'Well I'd contact her and say, "Can you wait till the end of the season?" And if you love her, go home and marry her.'

'I'm going to go home and marry her,' he said. 'I'll be there for the birth.'

'Well good. You're doing the right thing by Shirley.'

'But I'm not getting married until you come back at the end of the season,' Wewak said. 'You've got to be my best man.'

Well they never got married at the end of that year, like he'd said they would, but Wewak and Shirley were solid as a rock. Nine kids, fourteen grandchildren, and six great-grandchildren, the last time I counted.

It's funny you know – a similar thing happened with my brother John, John Paterson. He was a good footballer too. Played for the Buffaloes, and in later years became the president there. I was always keen to see if any of the Territory boys might be able to make it with me at West Perth. And I organised for John to come down and try out. But he finished up having to go back for personal reasons too.

But back to Wewak. In 2007, I get a call from his eldest son, David Junior. 'Uncle, you're going to get a call from Dad.'

'Oh yes, what about?'

'Don't say anything, don't say that I told you, but Mum and Dad are getting married.'

'Oh bullshit!'

So at the age of sixty-five, only forty-three years after it was supposed to happen, if you don't mind, I got to be the best man at the wedding of the number two grandson of George and Alice Holtze, my first cousin and lifetime mate, David Wewak Ross. And a jolly good time was had by all!

~

BUT THE REAL loose end that I finally managed to give proper attention to was my Alice Springs connection, the Dempsey family of my father Willie.

I knew the Dempsey story from Mum, of course. The two Irish brothers, Jack and John, who'd come to Alice Springs. Jack marrying a local woman and having three kids, Lilly and Ivy, and my father Willie. Lilly had stayed on in the Alice, but Ivy, the youngest, had been taken away by the Catholics and sent to Melville Island.

Other people used to tell me I had an Auntie Dorothy, and I'd tell them they didn't know what they were talking about, that was my Mum. But it turned out that, for reasons unknown, the Catholics changed Ivy's name to Dorothy when they took her away to the islands. So for a time, there were two Dorothy Dempseys floating around. Then my Auntie Dorothy married an Italian feller and became Dorothy Berto. It all got a bit confusing.

Then one day, I'm at a funeral in Katherine and Mum tells me to go over and talk to this woman that I didn't know. She was all over me. It turned out it was my Auntie Ivy, who'd become Dorothy Berto, and she hadn't seen me since I was a baby until that day.

After that, I'd see her from time to time in Darwin, without ever being real close to her, until one day, she had this big family barbecue that I was invited to. Everyone got talking about all the history and connections, and at one point, she leaned over and whispered to me, 'You haven't seen your father's grave, have you?' Willie was her brother of course. She didn't say it in a bad way, not at all, she was just saying. But it got me thinking.

This was around the mid 2000s. I was well into my sixties. And it was true. I hadn't seen my father's grave, and there were a whole lot of relations there in Alice Springs who I'd never met. So I went to Alice.

I met up with my cousins, Ian and Helen; their mother was Lilly, Willie's other sister. They told me how they used to follow my footy career at West Perth, which made me feel good. Ian was a big one for family history. He filled me in on all sorts of family stuff: the Alice Springs Dempseys, and the Mount Isa Dempseys. That's where the other Irish Dempsey brother, John, had finished up. He also lived with an Aboriginal woman, and there was a whole mob of us over there. Courtenay Dempsey who played for Essendon, came from that branch of the family.

Talking with Ian and Helen made me think about all the people and all the things and possibilities I'd missed out on, thanks to being taken away. About how different life might have been for me.

And then there was my main mission, finding my father's grave. I went to the council offices there. I told them my name, and that I was looking for William Dempsey's grave, unmarked, in the old cemetery. They looked it up. They had this map – letters, A, B, C, D and so on, down one side, and numbers down the other side.

They found him, William Dempsey, and showed me on the map whereabouts he was.

And then they said, 'There's also a Jack Dempsey here.'

'That's my grandfather.'

'And there's also a Patricia Dempsey.'

'That's my sister.'

They were all there. My father, my grandfather and my baby sister. All in unmarked graves in different sections of that old cemetery.

I went out there and I found them, all three of them.

I sat out there in that cemetery that night, with a bottle of red wine. It was very, very emotional. And it was spooky. From when I was a kid, my Granny Alice had filled my head with stories of the spirits of the Aboriginal world, and that night there amongst all those unmarked graves, with my head full of memories, I was seeing spirits and ghosts. I think my cousin Helen was getting a bit worried about me.

I rang up Josh. He was in Melbourne then, working for Ansett. He came up and met me there in Alice. I showed him the graves and I introduced him to all of his relations in the red centre.

I think I said something earlier on about having all these different circles of family. Up until then, although I couldn't really tell you why, I'd never really connected up with that particular circle, my father's people. It was a strange trip in some ways. I still get the shivers when I think of that night at the cemetery. But it was an important thing for me to do.

THIRTY-SEVEN

THE BIG WIGS at the Department were quite surprised that the program was run the way it was. No one had ever done it like that before. But they backed us for a long time. Us five managers worked as a team, and swapped notes and ideas all the time, and helped each other out where we had to. I worked with a community near Port Hedland at one stage and helped out at another one in the Goldfields.

We did a lot of work at Mowanjum. Jim Greatorex was the supervisor there. There was a real hotchpotch of buildings there, different styles of houses built at different times. Some of the oldest ones – there were seven or so of them – were in shocking condition. One of them just had a big pig living in it. Jim had been there about a year, and they were talking about starting on these houses.

Jimbo said, 'I've been thinking about it. Instead of just band-aiding it up, I reckon we've got to completely strip it, back to the frames.'

'Jeez, d'you really want to do that?'

'Yes. We can do it, I've been looking at it.'

'All right. If you reckon you can handle it, I'll support you and the boys.'

And they did it, stripped it right back to just the steel frame on the concrete pad and rebuilt it right from scratch. You should've seen it, just like a brand-new house. I loved it. I got them to do two more and kept a really close record of all the costings: wages, materials, you name it. It was costing us $82,000 a house, for what were actually brand-new houses.

At the same time, the Department of Housing had let out a contract to build three brand-new houses at Mowanjum. The work on them was going on at the same time as Jim and his team were doing the rebuilds. When I got down to Perth, I made a point of doing some digging and asking around. The brand-new ones cost $175,000 each compared to $82,000 each for our three. And for the families moving into them, it was exactly the same thing in effect either way: a brand-new house to live in. And the wages from ours stayed in the community at the same time as we were skilling up the locals.

ONCE WORD GOT around and people saw what we did, everyone wanted to be in on the Management Services Program. Because they used to watch the contractors come in, do the work, get paid and piss off, without ever listening to the community people. Contractors being contractors, you might say. But there was never enough money in the program to put on all the communities that wanted to take part.

All the blokes, especially in Fitzroy, used to tell me, 'That contractor mob, they don't like you, because we're doing all our own work.'

'Stuff them,' I'd say. 'I don't give a stuff about them. You mob, you're doing the right thing.'

And they were right. We weren't popular in some quarters. I used to hear it directly from them myself at a bar in

Fitzroy or Derby from time to time. They reckoned we were pinching their work.

And gradually, the money for the program started to get cut back and things became tougher. From 75 per cent Aboriginal staff in the Directorate, the numbers started to drop right back. The feeling I got was that the white people didn't like it. I think it was a bit of jealousy. So slowly, slowly, they killed it. People would say to me later, 'What happened to that program?'

All I could answer was, 'Circumstances.'

IT WAS THE first time I ever worked for the government, and I took it on reluctantly. I had no choice at the time and so I accepted. But in the end, I did that job for nearly twenty years. It was the longest stint of my life. Longer than Humes, longer than Dempsey Day, longer than my footy playing career even.

And I loved it. Because you could see people believing in themselves. They got their pride and their dignity back. You were helping people to help themselves.

THIRTY-EIGHT

I stayed with the Department of Housing, under all the different names it had, until I reached retirement age and it was a job I was pleased and proud to do.

I can officially claim to be an old feller now, I reckon, or an elder as we say in the Aboriginal world. I don't know about getting wiser as you get older, but I've certainly accumulated a few experiences, and a story or two to tell, and I'm doing okay as the years roll by. Mind you, I can't wear thongs anymore. They keep lopping off my toes one by one. That's thanks to the diabetes and poor circulation.

Up until recently, I was involved in getting a scheme up and running for a group of us elders to go into the prisons around Perth and mentor Aboriginal prisoners as they are approaching their release date, trying to help them with any issues they might have, and offer them what advice we can, to give them the best chance of surviving okay when they come out of detention.

I live a pretty quiet life these days with Jeran. But I still get to most of the West Perth games up at Joondalup, or South Geraldton as I like to call it. I've come to terms okay with the change to the Falcons, but I can't help but still think of them as the Cardies – the Cardinals as they were when I first pulled on the red and blue in 1960. On that subject, I should perhaps mention in passing that I'm not a fan of the idea of changing the club's name to the Joondalup Falcons. I've told Whinney – I can give him orders because I'm six months older than him – that if they do that, he's got to come and hold the ladder while I get up and take our names off the grandstand there that they named after us.

I still catch up with some of my old Cardie mates at a coffee club we do once a month, and I do lunches with J.J. Miller, the jockey, and some of the old footballers at an Italian restaurant down in Fremantle pretty regularly. And those two rascals Stan Hart and Ron Biok who I hooked up with when we were three young bucks in a Leederville boarding house are still good mates and good company.[1]

Mind you, that's all on hold as I wrap these stories up. It is the time of the Covid virus and we're all in lockdown. So far, I haven't driven Jeran completely mad.

WHEN YOU GET to my age, you tend to spend more time looking back over your life, rather than forward to what's still to come. That, and you find yourself going to too many funerals. I've buried more people dear to me than I care to remember. Grandpa George Holtze. And a few years after him, my Grandma Alice – Moondoolooloo.

In 2007, my dear old Mum passed away. There was a big gathering of the clan for that one and I was pleased that all of my kids except one were able to make it there to see her off.

1 Stan Hart passed away on 19th October 2020 as this book was in the final stages of preparation, to the great sorrow of Bill and Ron, and his family.

A few years back, even Jimmy 'the King' Anderson went to meet his maker. He was a tough bugger Jimmy, I thought he might outlast me. I miss him still, but he's there in my memories, and in most of my stories.

And Maxie, the brother boy who worked alongside me for sixteen years at Dempsey Day Scaffolding. The ranks of the old Retta Dixon brother boys and sister girls are thinning.

I spend more time remembering and thinking about all these good folk than I do remembering footy games. Especially my Mum. She is in so many of my stories and my memories. She was the roughest of rough diamonds, with a turn of phrase that could make the devil blush, and she was never one for taking a backward step. Our relationship may have been a difficult one and sometimes a strange one. We were always fighting, and I was almost as stubborn as she was. But she was a strong and inspirational woman and a powerful influence on my life, for the good. We always loved one another.

I do look back on my football career as well, and I do so with pride. My two clubs, the Darwin Buffaloes and the West Perth Cardinals, are etched deep in my heart. The best memories are the premierships, three with each club, because they are what you strive for with the guys you run out with each week, the teammates who become your friends, your comrades.

I'm also proud to have been an offsider and a partner of Graham Polly Farmer, the best player the game has seen, in two of those premierships. His daughter Kim is a bit young for me to call her a sister girl, but she has become like family to me and has ridden me all the way to make sure I put these stories down.

~

AS I LOOK back, I can tell you, straight-up, that I think of myself as a lucky man. That little boy who walked in the gates of the Retta Dixon Home on Bagot Road in Darwin with one little suitcase, who'd lost his father and sister, and thought his mother had abandoned him, has turned out to have a pretty good innings.

I'll tell you why I think I'm lucky.

It's not the footy.

It's not the fact that I escaped the fate those government men I eavesdropped on at Retta Dixon had planned for me as a shit ringer or a road worker. After all, there have been two men whose advice I have valued above just about all others in my life. One, my grandfather George, was a shit ringer. The other, my old mentor Froggie Snape, was a Darwin garbo.

It's family.

Most people only have one circle of people they think of as family. The number of people in that circle is different for everyone, from just a handful, up to dozens and dozens. Me, I've got family coming out my ears.

There's my blood family, Mum and my brothers and sisters and nieces and nephews, and all the Holtze descendants, and the Dempsey clan from Alice Springs, who I also got to know over the years. It could've been so different. Things didn't turn out well for so many of the stolen generations who, like me, grew up in institutions.

Then the institution I did grow up in provided another family for me. Again, for so many Aboriginal kids who were put into homes, it didn't turn out nearly so well. But us Retta Dixon kids made it work, by our own efforts. The brother boys and sister girls of Retta Dixon have been a great big family to me throughout my life.

I had some good years with Julie, and now I've got Jeran with me.

There's Josh, a son to be proud of, and his three beautiful kids, who seem happy enough to put up with their Grandpa.

There's those four girls who entered my life as surprises down the track.

Like I said, I've been lucky; I've got more family than most to turn to.

This Buffalo boy can look back on his life with a smile.

POSTSCRIPT

I'VE TOLD THE story of taking my son Josh back to Birdum, the place where I was born. He also wanted to see the place where I grew up. I drove him down Bagot Road there in Darwin, and showed him the spot. But there's nothing there any more.

We're all country and western fans, us old Territorians. It put me in mind of an old song that Hank Williams recorded, that I've taken some liberties with.

Memories of old Retta Dixon Home

I went to the old home
Where I once used to roam
And all of my playmates
Brothers and sisters
And everything gone
How sad and how drear
No voices did I hear
There was no one to welcome me home

I went to the old church
Where we all used to pray
Nothing was left and everything gone
How sad and how drear
No noise could I hear
There was nothing to welcome me home

ACKNOWLEDGEMENTS

I WOULD LIKE to acknowledge and thank the families who have been a part of my life:

The Holtze family
The Dempsey family of Alice Springs
The Patersons
The Georges
The Fejos
and the Hayes.
All the Retta Dixon brother boys and sister girls.
The Hart and Biok families.
The Buffaloes, and the West Perth Cardies.

Bill Dempsey

This book has been a long time in the making. There are many people who helped to make it possible. Thanks to the West Australian Football Commission, and the organisations and individuals who contributed financially. To Kim Farmer, who was tenacious in making sure that it happened, and the team who got behind her, including Michelle Broun, David

Milroy and Ernie Dingo, and the East Perth Football Club. To the West Perth Football Club for their assistance and support, and in particular to Peter and Nicole Cutler. To the State Library of Western Australia, particularly their volunteer Joe Blake for the huge and invaluable task of transcribing our research interviews, and their researcher Carol Smith for assistance at a time when Covid made it impossible to physically go to the library. To Dennis Cometti, Mal Brown and Mel Whinnen for their contributions.

Thanks to all the team at Magabala, and to West Australian Newspapers and all the others who contributed the photographs that add so much to the book.

Thanks to Jeran and to Lesley.

Bill Dempsey and *Steve Hawke*

PHOTOGRAPHS

For their assistance in sourcing and compiling the photographs, we would like to thank the following people and organisations: The Retta Dixon Home Association, Delean Hotze and Aunty Valerie Day; Deb Bisa; Don Christopherson; Peter Cutler; the Northern Territory Library; Ron Biok; Melissa Hayward at Westpix; and Jason Oliphant at West Australian Newspapers.

William (Bill) Dempsey MBE is a former Australian rules footballer who played for the Darwin (Buffaloes) Football Club in the Northern Territory Football League (NTFL) and the West Perth Football Club (Cardinals) in the Western Australian National Football League (WANFL). Born in Birdum (NT), and descended from the Jingili, Warramunga and Ngalakan peoples, Bill Dempsey is an inductee of both the AFL Northern Territory and the West Australian Football Halls of Fame.

Steve Hawke grew up in Melbourne, then lived in the Kimberley for many years before settling in the Perth hills. He has worked with a wide range of Kimberley Indigenous communities and organisations for over forty years. He has written plays, novels, a children's novel, biographies and social histories, including *A Town Is Born: The Fitzroy Crossing Story* for Magabala Books.